1999 Revised
1999年 修订

经贸初级汉语口语
BUSINESS CHINESE (ELEMENTARY)

上 册
BOOK ONE

黄为之 编著

华语教学出版社
SINOLINGUA

中国国家汉办赠送
Donated by Hanban, China

First Edition   1999
Second Printing 2002

All rights reserved. No part of this book may be reproduced, stored in a retrieval system, or transmitted in any form or by any means without permission in writing from the publisher.

ISBN 7-80052-705-0
Copyright 1999 by Sinolingua
Published by Sinolingua
24 Baiwanzhuang Road, Beijing 100037, China
Tel: (86) 10-68995871 / 68326333
Fax: (86) 10-68326333
E-mail: hyjx@263.net
Printed by Beijing Foreign Languages Printing House
Distributed by China International
Book Trading Corporation
35 Chegongzhuang Xilu, P.O. Box 399
Beijing 100044, China

Printed in the People's Republic of China

再版 前言

《经贸初级汉语口语》，1993年出版后，受到社会各界的热烈欢迎，被各院校和自学者广泛采用。出版六年来，中国的国际贸易形势发生了很大变化，有许多新的内容、新的语言需要学习；在教学实践中，我们也积累了经验，听取了各方面的意见，觉得对这本口语教材，现在进行修订、再版，是适时的。

1999年新版《经贸初级汉语口语》，在保持初版体例和优点的基础上，作了较大的全面修改。全书从原来的36课增加到50课，由一册分为上、下册，原有的内容作了调整，增加了经贸领域出现的新话题、新词语；减缓了学习进程的坡度，由浅入深、循序渐进的教学原则，得到了更充分的体现。我们相信，这个新版本，会在更高的水准上满足教师和学习者的需要。

1999年新版《经贸初级汉语口语》的英语翻译是黄震华教授。

对外经济贸易大学
黄为之
1999年2月

Preface to the 1999 Edition

Since its publication in 1993, *Business Chinese* (*Elementary*) has been well-received by various circles of the society, and adopted as textbook by various universities and colleges and self-taught learners. The situation of China's international business has witnessed great changes during the past six years, which means that there are lots of new things to learn. In our teaching practice, we have also accumulated experiences and listened to suggestions from all sources. We feel that it is the right time now to revise and republish this book.

The 1999 edition of *Business Chinese* (*Elementary*), while keeping the format and merits of the first edition, has undergone major and comprehensive revision. The number of lessons has been increased to 50 from 36, and the new edition appears in two volumes. The contents have also been enriched, with new topics and new expressions in the arena of business and economics added, and the slope of the degree of difficulty lowered so that the principle of proceeding step by step from the easy to the difficult is better exemplified. We believe that the new edition will be better able to meet the needs of the teachers and learners.

The English translator of the 1999 edition of *Business Chinese (Elementary)* is Professor Huang Zhenhua.

Huang Weizhi
University of International
Business and Economics,
February, 1999

原版 前言

本教材的适用对象是从零开始的初学者。

留学生学习汉语有他们自身的特殊性。一方面,他们对汉语一无所知,没有听说汉语的能力;另一方面,他们又大多是成年人,有充分发达的智能,丰富的社会阅历和科学知识;他们没有孩子那样强的语言模仿力,而同时又具有孩子无可比拟的理解力和接受力。留学生的这个特殊性,在汉语学习过程中,形成一对突出的矛盾。它一方面要求教师注意学生零起点特点,必须象教孩子学话一样,从一字一词教起,学生也必须从一字一词学起,学习必然存在着一个日积月累,循序渐进的过程;另一方面,它又要求教师充分注意到学生的成人特点,在教学过程中,不要把学生简单地当学话的孩子对待,而应该运用各种手段调动学生的主观能动性,发挥他们的智能、阅历和知识优势,使他们既学得扎实,又学得快捷。如何认识留学生学习汉语的这种特殊性,并把这种认识运用在教材编写和教学过程中,过去往往被人们忽略。教学内容和教学进度的超前或滞后,是常有的现象。我在编写这本初级口语时,考虑到上述情况,试图解决好留学生在学习汉语中存在的这种矛盾性,使教与学都取得最理想的效果。

本教材具有下面一些特点:

一至四课集中学习汉语拼音,这是为零起点的初学者编写的。来自东方国家的留学生,声母和韵母的发音难点较多;而来自西方国家的留学生,声调语调的问题则较突出。这四课中,有针对性地编入了大量练习。五至十课,还有拼音练习,以巩固前四课的学习成果。通过严格的教学实践,学生就可以比较好地解决这些语音问题,为学好标准的普通话打下坚实基础。

本教材是经贸专业汉语教材。教材内容与常见的普通汉语教材内容有极大不同。普通汉语教材中,日常衣食住行和校园生活内容,占有相当大比重,本教材则把其中的有用部分与日常经济生活巧妙地结合了起来,而以经济生活为主要内容。日常经济生活,包括买卖东西、讨价还价、货物挑选、商业服务、销售广告、经营特色、公关工作、推销技巧等,内容丰富,涉及面广,切近生活,实际有用,而教材的词汇、句型及难易程度,又都与初学者的实际水平相当。

本教材根据语言有交际情景与交际功能属性的原理,采用了课内与课外相结合的教学体系。从第五课开始,每两课一个专题。换句话说,我把日常经济生活,分为若干个层面,每一个层面,都用两篇课文来认识它,表述它。课文"在课内",是在教师指导下的学习。这是闭门操练,务求根基扎实。课文"在课外",是学生走出课堂,参与社会实践。这是亲自下海,在游泳中学游泳,意在复习和运用课堂学到的语言知识。两篇课文,内容紧密相关而天地各不相同。学生学完并掌握了这两篇课文,也就学到了经济生活中一个层面的日常用语。这种教学体系,冲出了封闭式的课堂。教师在组织每一个专题课时,都可以要求学生在课前或课后,去参加相应的社会实践,为这一个专题的教学做课前准备或课后复习。本教材在进入教学过程后,必将以它生动活泼的教学形式,引起学生的极大兴趣,充分调动起学习积极性,发挥出成年人的学习优势,取得预期的效果。

本教材在教学安排上,采用了低起点,大容量,高密度,分阶段而又大步推进的强化训练教学法。每一篇课文,生词量和篇幅长度，都超出了常见的同级普通汉语课本；整个教学过程，都以学生为主，课内课外的一切活动，都要求学生主动积极地去完成，教师只是参与、启发、引导，而决不做教授式的讲演。教学活动的单调、缓慢，学生学习的被动、疲塌，都是影响教学质量的不利因素。本教材提供了强化训练的丰富素材和各种手段，教师可以充分利用这些素材和手段，激发学生的强烈学习欲望和潜在能力，使学生进入学习的兴奋状态和紧张状态。我所说的"紧张状态"，绝不排斥生动活泼、趣味盎然的教学气氛。恰恰相反，这种教学气氛越浓，学生也就越兴奋，越投入，知识的学习与运用也就越能达到最佳境界，一切看似不可能一下学会的东西，就有可能在最短的时间里学到手，甚至运用得熟巧。

这本教材，从内容到形式，都走了一条新路子，肯定是不完善，不成熟的，还需要在今后的教学实践中作更深入的探索，希望能听到同行教师和留学生们的批评意见。

本教材由我校副校长黄震华教授负责全书的英文注释和翻译。加拿大籍专家 David Packer 先生校阅了课文译文。我校校长孙维炎教授最后审定了全书。国家对外汉语教学领导小组办公室的领导同志，对本教材的编写与出版给予了指导和帮助。我校校领导、出版社和外事处的同志们，都给本教材的出版以大力支持。在此，我对他们表示由衷的感谢。

对外经济贸易大学
黄为之
1993 年 1 月

Preface to the First Edition

This textbook is meant for beginners.

Foreign students learning the Chinese language have their own specific characteristics. On the one hand, they know nothing about Chinese, and they do not have the listening comprehension and speaking abilities concerning this target language. On the other, most of them are adults with fully-developed intellects, rich social experience and scientific knowledge. They do not have as strong a language imitation ability as small children, but at the same time, they have an understanding and receptive ability with which small children cannot compare. These characteristics are, in a way, contradictory. Teachers are required to pay attention to the fact that their students are starting from scratch, and they have to begin their teaching from simple words, just like teaching small children to speak. Students have to start their learning from simple words too. The learning process is one of gradual accumulation. The characteristics of the learners also require the teachers to pay attention to the fact that their students are adults, and not to treat them like small children. They have to use every means to bring the students' initiative into full play, mobilizing their superiority in intelligence, experience and knowledge, so that they can learn solid knowledge quickly. The question of how to understand the special characteristics of foreign students learning Chinese and to utilize such knowledge in the compilation of textbooks and in the teaching process has often been neglected. It has frequently been the case that the content and speed of teaching has been either too advanced or lagging behind. In writing this elementary Chinese conversation book, I have taken these aspects into consideration, trying to resolve the aforementioned contradictions in the process of foreign students' learning Chinese, so as to bring about the most satisfactory results in both learning and teaching.

The present textbook has the following characteristics:

Lessons one to four concentrate on the learning of the Chinese phonetic alphabet or *pinyin*. This is for the benefit of beginners. Students coming from Oriental countries have more difficulties in the pronunciation of vowels and consonants, while those from Western countries have their main problems in tones and intonation. These four lessons contain a large number of exercises directed at such problems. Phonological exercises continue in lessons five to ten, with a view to consolidating what was learned in the first four lessons. Through strict learning and teaching practice, students can solve these phonological problems, laying a solid foundation for mastering standard *putonghua* (the common dialect).

The purpose of the present textbook is to teach Chinese on

international business, the content of which is very different from those of ordinary textbooks, where a large proportion is devoted to such daily matters as food, clothing, shelter and transportation, and to life in campus. The present book endeavours to combine the useful parts of the previously mentioned topics with those daily business routines such as buying and selling, bargaining, selection of goods, commercial services, advertising, special features of management, public relations, salesmanship, etc. Emphasis is placed on these aspects and the content is such that the students are exposed to a broad range of knowledge that is realistic and practical. The book's vocabulary, sentence structures, and level of difficulty are suitable for beginners.

According to the principle that language has such properties as communicative situation and communicative functions, the present book has adopted a system of combining learning in class and out of class. Starting from lesson five (lesson 11 of the 1999 edition), there are two lessons for each topic. More specifically, I have divided daily business life into several strata, each of which is presented in two lessons. The "in class" text is for learning under the teacher's guidance. It is closed-door practice, aimed at laying a solid foundation. The "out of class" text is for students to learn when they participate in social practice. In the vernacular, we might say this is "going into the sea and learning how to swim by swimming". Its purpose is to review and use the linguistic knowledge that has been learned in class. The content of the two texts is closely related, but with different fields of activity. When the students have learned and mastered both texts, they have also learned the daily expressions for one stratum of "economic life". This teaching system has broken down the closed classroom approach. In organizing the teaching of a topic, the teacher can always ask the students to take part in the corresponding social practice either before or after class, as a preview or review of the theme. After entering into the teaching process, the present textbook, with its active and lively teaching style, will arouse great interest from the students, motivate them to learn, and take into account the extraordinary learning capabilities of adults, so as to achieve the expected results.

The present textbook starts with basic greetings, and, through careful yet intensive introduction of key vocabulary and expressions, moves through successive stages so that the number of new words and the length of the texts have both exceeded those of the ordinary Chinese textbooks. The whole teaching process is student-centred. Students are required to accomplish both the in-class and the after-class activities before they proceed. The teacher's role is to participate, inspire, and guide, but never lecture. The monotony and slow pace in the teaching and learning activities, and the passiveness and slackness on the part of the students are negative factors affecting the learning result. The present book has provided ample materials and means for intensive training, which can be fully utilized by the teachers to stimulate the students' strong desire and potential to learn. Students respond to a lively and interesting learning atmosphere. The better the learning atmosphere, the more excited and involved the students will become. Hence the optimal state will be attained for learning and use of knowledge. Things that seem impossible to learn will be mastered within the shortest possible time.

As this book has followed a new path in both its content and form, errors are inevitable. Further exploration is needed in teaching and learning a language. Therefore, criticisms and suggestions from fellow teachers and foreign students are most welcome.

The English translation of all the texts and explanations has been done by Professor Huang Zhenhua, vice president of our University. Mr David Packer, a Canadian expert working at our University, assisted with the English translation. And finally Professor Sun Weiyan, president of our University, examined the manuscript of the whole book. Senior members from the Office of the Leading Group for the Teaching of Chinese to Foreign Learners have provided guidance and support for the compilation and publication of the present book. Leading members of our University, and colleagues from our University Press and Foreign Affairs Office have also given substantial support to this book. I hereby extend my heartfelt thanks to all of them.

        Huang Weizi
        at the University of International
        Business and Economics
        January, 1993

目录
Contents

普通话声韵拼合总表
Table of the Combinations of the Initials and Finals in Common Speech

第一课	你好 ……………………	1
Lesson 1	Hello	
第二课	他是谁 ……………………	13
Lesson 2	Who Is He	
第三课	我的朋友 ……………………	25
Lesson 3	My Friends	
第四课	怎么称呼 ……………………	37
Lesson 4	How to Call a Person	
第五课	打电话 ……………………	48
Lesson 5	Making Telephone Calls	
第六课	预订房间 ……………………	58
Lesson 6	Booking a Room	
第七课	换钱 ……………………	66
Lesson 7	Changing Money	
第八课	出租车 ……………………	75
Lesson 8	Taxi	

第九课	他没来上班 ………………………	85
Lesson 9	He Has Not Turned Up for Work	
第十课	今天是她的生日 ……………………	94
Lesson 10	It Is Her Birthday Today	
第十一课	你想做什么(一) ………………………	105
Lesson 11	What Do You Want to Do (1)	
第十二课	你想做什么(二) ………………………	114
Lesson 12	What Do You Want to Do (2)	
第十三课	你会说中国话吗(一) …………………	122
Lesson 13	Do You Speak Chinese (1)	
第十四课	你会说中国话吗(二) …………………	131
Lesson 14	Do You Speak Chinese (2)	
第十五课	你会买东西吗(一) ……………………	139
Lesson 15	Do You Know How to Make Purchases (1)	
第十六课	你会买东西吗(二) ……………………	149
Lesson 16	Do You Know How to Make Purchases (2)	
第十七课	她怎么了(一) …………………………	158
Lesson 17	What's the Matter with Her (1)	
第十八课	她怎么了(二) …………………………	168
Lesson 18	What's the Matter with Her (2)	
第十九课	是谁的错(一) …………………………	178
Lesson 19	Whose Fault Is It (1)	
第二十课	是谁的错(二) …………………………	189
Lesson 20	Whose Fault Is It (2)	
第二十一课	住在哪儿(一) ………………………	199
Lesson 21	Where Are You Staying (1)	

第二十二课	住在哪儿(二)	208
Lesson 22	Where Are You Staying (2)	
第二十三课	今天怎么样(一)	217
Lesson 23	What's the Weather like Today (1)	
第二十四课	今天怎么样(二)	225
Lesson 24	What's the Weather like Today (2)	
第二十五课	逛北京(一)	234
Lesson 25	Roaming Around Beijing (1)	
第二十六课	逛北京(二)	245
Lesson 26	Roaming Around Beijing (2)	
英译课文		257
English Translation of the Texts		
生词总表		294
Vocabulary List		

第一课　你好
Lesson 1　Hello

学拼音 xué pīnyīn
The Phonetic Alphabet（1）

一、**韵母**（yùnmǔ）Vowels

  a o e i u ü

声母（一）(shēngmǔ) Consonants

  b p m f d t n l

1. 拼读练习（pīn dú liànxí）Combine sounds into syllables：

	a	o	e	i	u	ü
b	ba	bo		bi	bu	
p	pa	po		pi	pu	
m	ma	mo	me	mi	mu	
f	fa	fo			fu	
d	da		de	di	du	
t	ta		te	ti	tu	
n	na		ne	ni	nu	nü
l	la		le	li	lu	lü

2. 辨音练习（biàn yīn liànxí）Distinguish the sounds：

ba——pa	bo——po	bi——pi	bu——pu
da——ta	de——te	di——ti	du——tu
na——la	ne——le	ni——li	nu——lu
nü——lü			

声母（二）（shēngmǔ）Consonants

j q x g k h

1. 拼读练习（pīndú liànxí）Combine sounds into syllables：

	a	o	e	i	u	ü
j				ji		ju
q				qi		qu
x				xi		xu
g	ga		ge		gu	
k	ka		ke		ku	
h	ha		he		hu	

2. 辨音练习（biàn yīn liànxí）Distinguish the sounds：

ji——ju	ji——qi	ji——xi
ju——qu	ju——xu	qu——xu
qi——xu	qi——xi	qi——qu
xi——ju	xi——qu	xi——xu

ga——ka	ge——ke	gu——ku
ka——ha	ke——he	ku——hu
ha——ga	he——ge	hu——gu
ga——ge	ke——ku	he——hu

韵母二、(yùnmǔ) Vowels：

　　　ai　ei　ao　ou
　　　an　en　ang　eng　ong

1. 拼读练习 (pīndú liànxí) Combine sounds into syllables：

	ai	ei	ao	ou	an	en	ang	eng	ong
b	bai	bei	bao		ban	ben	bang	beng	
p	pai	pei	pao	pou	pan	pen	pang	peng	
m	mai	mei	mao	mou	man	men	mang	meng	
f		fei		fou	fan	fen	fang	feng	
d	dai	dei	dao	dou	dan	den	dang	deng	dong
t	tai		tao	tou	tan		tang	teng	tong
n	nai	nei	nao	nou	nan	nen	nang	neng	nong
l	lai	lei	lao	lou	lan		lang	leng	long
j									
q									
x									
g	gai	gei	gao	gou	gan	gen	gang	geng	gong
k	kai	kei	kao	kou	kan	ken	kang	keng	kong
h	hai	hei	hao	hou	han	hen	kang	heng	hong

2. 辨音练习 (biàn yīn liànxí) Distinguish the sounds：

　　bai——pai　bei——pei　bao——pao　ban——pan
　　dai——tai　dao——tao　dou——tou　dan——tan
　　nai——lai　nao——lao　nou——lou　nan——lan
　　gai——kai　gao——kao　gou——kou　gan——kan
　　bang——pang　beng——peng
　　dang——tang　deng——teng　dong——tong
　　gang——kang　geng——keng　gong——kong

声调练习、(shēngdiào liànxí) Get the tones right:

ā á ǎ à
ō ó ǒ ò
ē é ě è
ī í ǐ ì
ū ú ǔ ù
ǖ ǘ ǚ ǜ

mā má mǎ mà
bā bá bǎ bà
dī dí dǐ dì
gē gé gě ·gè
nī ní nǐ nì
wō wó wǒ wò
yē yé yě yè
hēn hén hěn hèn
hāo háo hǎo hào

课文
Text

A：你好！
B：你好！

A：小姐，你好！
B：你好！

A：嗨，安娜，你好！
B：你好，杰克！

A：安娜，早上好！
B：早上好，杰克！

A：嗨，安娜！
B：嗨，杰克！
A：你好吗？
B：谢谢，我很好！你呢？
A：我也很好！

汉语拼音课文
Text in *Pinyin* (Phonetic Spelling)

A：Nǐ hǎo！
B：Nǐ hǎo！

A: Xiǎojie, nǐ hǎo!
B: Nǐ hǎo!

A: Hāi, Annà, nǐ hǎo!
B: Nǐ hǎo, Jiékè!

A: Annà, zǎoshang hǎo!
B: Zǎoshang hǎo, Jiékè!

A: Hāi, Annà!
B: Hāi, Jiékè!
A: Nǐ hǎo ma?
B: Xièxiè, Wǒ hěn hǎo! Nǐ ne?
A: Wǒ yě hěn hǎo!

生词
New Words

1. 你　　nǐ　　　　you
2. 好　　hǎo　　　good, fine, well
3. 小姐　xiǎojie　　Miss
4. 嗨　　hāi　　　hey
5. 早上　zǎoshang　morning
6. 吗　　ma　　　(auxiliary word, used at the end of a yes-no question)

7.	谢谢	xièxie	thank you, thanks
8.	我	wǒ	I, me
9.	很	hěn	very
10.	呢	ne	(auxiliary word, often used at the end of a wh-question)
11.	也	yě	too, also, as well, either

专名
Proper Nouns

| 安娜 | Annà | Anna |
| 杰克 | Jiékè | Jack |

注释
Notes

一、现代汉语可以用拼音记音。现代汉语拼音共有21个声母,38个韵母。汉语的音节大多是由声母和韵母拼合成的。有的音节,只有韵母,没有声母。

Modern Chinese uses the phonetic alphabet or *pinyin* to record the pronunciation. Its phonetic alphabet has 21 consonants and 38 vowels. Most Chinese syllables are formed by spelling consonants and vowels together. Some syllables have only vowels and no consonants.

二、声调:汉语的每一个音节都有声调,声调有区别语义的作用,相同的音节,声调不同,语义也不同。现代汉语普通话有四个基本声调,声调名称和符号是-(第一声),ʹ(第二声),ˇ(第三声),\(第四声)。各声调调值分别为:-(55),ʹ(35),ˇ(214),\(51),图示如下:

Tones: Every Chinese syllable has tones, which have the function of distinguishing meanings. *Putonghua* (the common dialect) of modern Chinese has four basic tones. The same syllable with different tones differs in meaning. The names and marks for these tones are: - (the first tone), ʹ (the second tone), ˇ (the third tone), \ (the fourth tone). The tone pitches of the four tones are as follows: - (55), ʹ (35), ˇ (214), and \ (51).

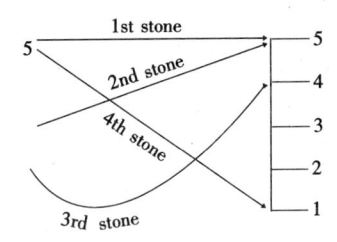

三、"吗、呢",都是语气助词。用"吗"表示疑问语气,可用在是非问句的末尾。例如:

吗 and 呢 are both auxiliary words. 吗 is used to mark the interrogative mood. It is placed at the end of a yes-no question.

　　A:你好吗?
　　B:我好。(我不好。)

用"呢"也可表示疑问语气,用在是非问句以外的问句。例如:
呢 also indicates the interrogative mood. It is used in a wh-question.

A:你好吗?
B:我很好。你呢?
A:我也很好。

四、本课课文有五组对话,是常用的五种问候方式。第一种,认识的人或不认识的人见面,都可以这样互致问候。第二种,用于问候不认识的人,称呼对方"小姐"、"先生",是对对方的尊敬,比较礼貌、客气。第三种,用于认识的朋友、同学、同事,所以可以称呼对方的名字。第四种,是西方国家的一种问候方式,但近年来,在中国,特别是在有文化的人中间,也流行起来。第五种,是用疑问句形式表达问候。

The text of this lesson consists of five dialogues, which are the five most common ways of greeting. The first is used either between strangers or between people who are acquainted with each other. The second is used to greet a stranger. To use "Miss", or "Mr." to address the other party is to show one's respect, which is more polite. The third is used between friends, fellow students, or colleagues. So you can call the other party by their given name. The fourth is a greeting common in the West, but it has become quite popular in China in recent years, especially between educated people. The last one is to use an interrogative sentence for greeting.

补充生词
Additional New Words

爸爸	bàba	father
妈妈	māma	mother

哥哥	gēge	elder brother
弟弟	dìdi	younger brother
姐姐	jiějie	elder sister
妹妹	mèimei	younger sister
先生	xiānsheng	Mister, gentleman, sir
老师	lǎoshī	teacher
下午	xiàwǔ	afternoon
晚上	wǎnshang	evening, night

练习
Exercises

一、替换练习：

Substitution drills：

A：<u>小姐</u>，你好！
B：你好！

先生	老师

A：你好，<u>杰克</u>！
B：你好！

安娜	姐姐
哥哥	妹妹

A：<u>安娜</u>，早上好！
B：早上好。

爸爸	妈妈
先生	老师

A：<u>杰克</u>，你好吗？
B：谢谢，我很好！你呢？
A：我也很好。

哥哥	姐姐
弟弟	爸爸
安娜	

二、用拼音写出不同问候方式并熟读：

Give the phonetic notation of greetings and memorize them：

三、为下列单词写拼音并组句熟读：

Give the phonetic notation of the following words, form them into sentences and memorize them：

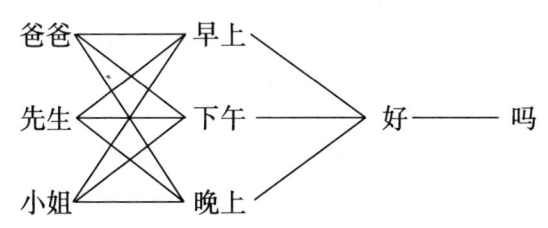

```
爸爸 ——— 早上
先生 ——— 下午 ———> 好 ——— 吗
小姐 ——— 晚上
```

四、为下图写拼音,组句：

Give the phonetic notation of the following, and use them to form sentences：

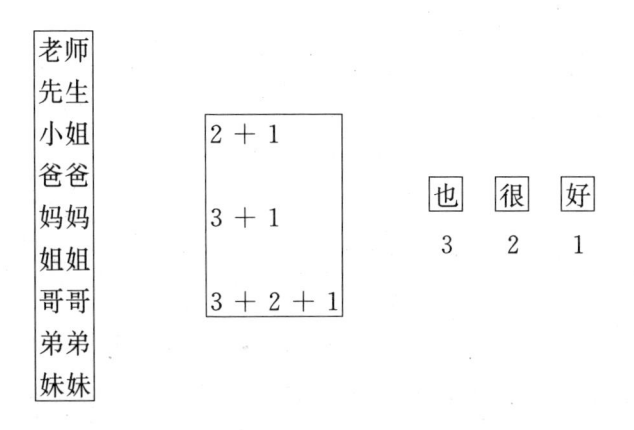

| 老师 |
| 先生 |
| 小姐 |
| 爸爸 |
| 妈妈 |
| 姐姐 |
| 哥哥 |
| 弟弟 |
| 妹妹 |

```
2 + 1

3 + 1

3 + 2 + 1
```

也	很	好
3	2	1

五、把下面的词组成句子：

Unscramble the following into normal sentences：

11

1. 你　小姐　好
2. 先生　好　早上
3. 很　好　我　也
4. 你　很　也　吗　好

六、写课内生词并注拼音。
Copy the new words and give the phonetic notation.

第二课　他是谁
Lesson 2　Who Is He

学拼音 xué pīnyīn
The Phonetic Alphabet (2)

一、声母 (shēngmǔ) Consonants

z　c　s　zh　ch　sh　r

1. 拼读练习（pīn dú liànxí）Combine sounds into syllables：

	a	o	e	-i	ai	ei	ong
z	za		ze	zi	zai	zei	zong
c	ca		ce	ci	cai		cong
s	sa		se	si	sai		song
zh	zha		zhe	zhi	zhai	zhei	zhong
ch	cha		che	chi	chai		chong
sh	sha		she	shi	shai	shei	
r			re	ri			rong

2. 辨音练习 (biàn yīn liànxí) Distinguish the sounds：

za——ca　　za——sa　　ca——sa
ze——ce　　ze——se　　ce——se

13

zi—ci zi—si ci—si cu—su
ri—ni zi—ji si—xi ru—nu

za—zha ze—zhe zi—zhi zu—zhu
ca—cha ce—che ci—chi cu—chu
sa—sha se—she si—shi su—shu

zao—zhao zou—zhou zan—zhan zeng—zheng
cai—chai cao—chao cou—chou cang—chang
sao—shao sou—shou san—shan seng—sheng

二、韵母 (yùnmǔ) Vowels

ia ie iao iou(iu)
ian in iang ing iong

1. 拼读练习 (pīn dú liànxí) Combine sounds into syllables：

	ia	ie	iao	iou	ian	in	iang	ing	iong
b		bie	biao		bian	bin		bing	
p		pie	piao		pian	pin		ping	
m		mie	miao	miu	mian	min		ming	
d		die	diao	diu	dian			ding	
t		tie	tiao		tian			ting	
n		nie	niao	niu	nian	nin	niang	ning	
l	lia	lie	liao	liu	lian	lin	liang	ling	
j	jia	jie	jiao	jiu	jian	jin	jiang	jing	jiong
q	qia	qie	qiao	qiu	qian	qin	qiang	qing	qiong
x	xia	xie	xiao	xiu	xian	xin	xiang	xing	xiong

2. 辨音练习 (biàn yīn liànxí) Distinguish the sounds:

bie——pie	biao——piao	bian——pian
die——tie	diao——tiao	dian——tian
jia——qia	jie——pie	jiu——qiu
bin——bing	pin——ping	min——ming
ding——ting	jing——qing	jiong——qiong
jiao——qiao	jian——qian	jiong——xiong

三、声调练习 (shēngdiào liànxí) Get the tones right:

qīng qíng qǐng qìng
wēn wén wěn wèn } qǐng wèn (we should like to ask)

zāi zái zǎi zài
jiān jián jiǎn jiàn } zài jiàn (goodbye)

zhōng zhóng zhǒng zhòng
guō guó guǒ guò } Zhōng guó (China)

bēi béi běi bèi
jīng jíng jǐng jìng } Běi jīng (Beijing)

xiē xié xiě xiè —— xiè xie (Thank you)
gù kè (customer)   miàn bāo (bread)
niú nǎi (milk)   qì chē (car)
tóng zhì (comrade)   qīn mì (intimate)
hòu tiān (day after tomorrow)   Xuě bì (Sprite)
zì diǎn (dictionary)   yǐ zi (chair)

课文
Text

A:你好！我是谢文。
B:你好！我是安娜。
A:很高兴认识你！
B:认识你,我也很高兴！

A:你是经理吗？
B:不,我是秘书,他是经理。
A:啊,对不起！
B:没关系！

A:经理,你好！我是安娜·李。
B:李小姐,你好！这是谁？
A:这是朱丽亚。
C:朱丽亚·利维,美国人。
B:你好！很高兴认识你！
C:认识你,我也很高兴！

A:经理,早上好！
B:早上好,安娜！
A:我是朱丽亚。
B:啊,对。你好,朱丽亚夫人！
A:小姐,朱丽亚·利维小姐。

B：啊，对不起，利维小姐！
A：没关系！

汉语拼音课文
Text in *Pinyin*

A：Nǐ hǎo! Wǒ shì Xiè Wén.
B：Nǐ hǎo! Wǒ shì Ānnà.
A：Hěn gāoxìng rènshi nǐ!
B：Rènshi nǐ, wǒ yě hěn gāoxìng!

A：Nǐ shì jīnglǐ ma?
B：Bù, wǒ shì mìshū, tā shì jīnglǐ.
A：À, duìbuqǐ!
B：Méi guānxi!

A：Jīnglǐ, nǐ hǎo! Wǒ shì Ānnà·Lǐ.
B：Lǐ xiǎojie, nǐ hǎo! Zhè shì shuí?
A：Zhè shì Zhūlìyà.
C：Zhūlìyà·Lìwéi, Měiguó rén.
B：Nǐ hǎo! Hěn gāoxìng rènshi nǐ!
C：Rènshi nǐ, wǒ yě hěn gāoxìng!

A：Jīnglǐ, zǎoshang hǎo!
B：Zǎoshang hǎo, Ānnà!

A：Wǒ shì Zhūlìyà.

B：À, duì. Nǐ hǎo, Zhūlìyà fūrén!

A：Xiǎojie, Zhūlìyà·Lìwéi xiǎojie.

B：À, duì bu qǐ, Lìwéi xiǎojie!

A：Méi guānxi!

生词
New Words

1.	这	zhè	this
2.	是	shì	be
3.	谁	shuí	who
4.	高兴	gāoxìng	glad, happy, pleased, cheerful
5.	认识	rènshi	know
6.	经理	jīnglǐ	manager
7.	不	bù	no, not
8.	秘书	mìshū	secretary
9.	他	tā	he, him
10.	啊	à	eh, oh, ah
11.	对	duì	right, correct
12.	对不起	duì bu qǐ	I'm sorry; excuse me; pardon me
13.	没关系	méi guānxi	it doesn't matter; that's all right; never mind
14.	人	rén	man, person, people, human

		being	
15. 夫人	fūren	wife, lady, Mrs., Madame	

专名
Proper Nouns

谢文	Xiè Wén	Xie Wen
朱丽亚·利维	Zhūlìyà·Lìwéi	Julia Levy

注释
Notes

一、注意单元音 i 和 -i〔ı〕的区别。i 是不圆唇的舌尖前元音。-i 是不圆唇舌尖后元音。同 zh、ch、sh、r 相拼合的是 -i, 单元音 i 永远不出现在 zh、ch、sh、r 之后。

Please note the distinction between the single vowel i and -i 〔ı〕. i is a non-rounded apical front vowel, and -i is a non-rounded apical back vowel. That which goes with zh, ch, sh and r is -i. The single vowel i never appears after zh, ch, sh or r.

二、现代汉语的声调,除四个基本声调外,还有一个轻声。轻声字不标调号,读时声音又轻又短。例如:

In modern Chinese, apart from the four basic tones, there is the light tone, which does not bear any tone marks and whose pronunciation should be both light and short.

爸爸　bàba

妈妈　　māma
小姐　　xiǎojie
先生　　xiānsheng
对不起　duì bu qǐ
没关系　méi guānxi

三、现代汉语普通话每一个音节的声调符号在书写时,都标在元音上方,当一个音节的韵母有两个或三个元音时,则标在开口度最大的元音上。如:hǎo、kǒu。

The tone mark for each syllable in *putonghua* of modern Chinese is written on top of the vowel. When a syllable has two or three vowels, it is placed on top of the vowel that is most open, e.g. hǎo, kǒu.

四、"是",动词,在句子中作谓语,表示一种肯定的判断。下面是汉语中最常见的一种句子格式:主语+谓语"是"+宾语。例如:

是 is a verb which, when functioning as the predicate in a sentence, expresses a positive judgment. The following is one of the most frequently used sentence patterns in Chinese: subject+是(the predicate verb)+predicative.

1. 我是安娜。
2. 他是经理。
3. 她是美国人。
4. 杰克也是美国人。

"是"的否定形式是在"是"的前面加否定副词"不"。例如:

The negative form of 是 is to put the negative adverb 不 before 是.

1. 她不是安娜。
2. 谢文不是经理。
3. 他不是老师。
4. 山口不是法国小姐。

补充生词
Additional New Words

学生	xuésheng	student
她	tā	she, her
哪	nǎ	which
国	guó	country, state, nation
中国	Zhōngguó	China
美国	Měiguó	the United States
英国	Yīngguó	the U.K.
法国	Fǎguó	France
俄罗斯	Éluósī	Russia
日本	Rìběn	Japan
韩国	Hánguó	Korea

练习
Exercises

一、替换练习：
Substitution drills：

A：他是谁？
B：他是<u>杰克</u>。
A：你好！<u>杰克</u>！很高兴认识你。
B：你好！我也很高兴认识你。

谢文	安娜
朱丽亚	经理
老师	

A：你是老师吗？
B：不，我是<u>经理</u>，他是<u>老师</u>。
A：对不起。
B：没关系。

杰克	谢文
秘书	经理
夫人	小姐

A：你是<u>美</u>国人吗？
B：不，我不是<u>美</u>国人，我是<u>英</u>国人。
A：认识你很高兴。
B：我也很高兴。

法国	俄罗斯
日本	韩国
日本	中国

二、完成对话：

Complete the following dialogues：

A：你是谁？
B：＿＿＿＿＿＿。
A：你是美国人吗？
B：＿＿＿＿＿＿。
A：你夫人是中国人吗？
B：＿＿＿＿＿＿。
A：对不起。
B：＿＿＿＿＿＿。
　小姐是哪国人？
A：＿＿＿＿＿＿。
B：认识你很高兴。
A：＿＿＿＿＿＿。

22

三、用下列词语填空、组句：

Put the following words into the blanks and form sentences according to the example：

例句：|妈妈|是|老师|,|爸爸|也是|老师|。

1. 先生　　夫人　　经理

2. 先生　　小姐　　美国人　　　　□是□,

3. 哥哥　　姐姐　　学生　　　　　□也是□。

4. 经理　　秘书　　日本人

例句：|妈妈|是|老师|,|爸爸|不是|老师|。

1. 爸爸　　哥哥　　经理

2. 姐姐　　妹妹　　秘书　　　　　□是□,

3. 先生　　小姐　　俄罗斯　　　　□不是□。

4. 安娜　　杰克　　法国

四、把下面的词组成句子：

Unscramble the following into normal sentences：

1. 我　你　认识　高兴　很

2. 也　我　你　很　认识　高兴

23

3. 经理　我　是　不

4. 吗　小姐　中国人　是

五、快速回答：

Give quick responses to the following：

1. 谁认识经理？

2. 经理是中国人吗？

3. 你高兴吗？

4. 我高兴,你呢？

5. 他很高兴,你呢？

六、写课内生词并注拼音。

Copy the new words and give the phonetic notation.

第三课　我的朋友
Lesson 3　My Friends

学拼音 xué pīnyīn
The Phoentic Alphabet (3)

一、韵母（yùnmǔ）Vowels

ua　uo　uai　uei　(ui)

uan　un　uang　ueng

üe　üan　ün

1. 拼读练习（pīn dú liànxí）Combine sounds into syllables：

	ua	uo	uai	ui	uan	un	uang	ueng
d		duo		dui	duan	dun		
t		tuo		tui	tuan	tun		
n		nuo			nuan			
l		luo			luan	lun		
z		zuo		zui	zuan	zun		
c		cuo		cui	cuan	cun		
s		suo		sui	suan	sun		

zh	zhua	zhuo	zhuai	zhui	zhuan	zhun	zhuang
ch	chua	chuo	chuai	chui	chuan	chun	chuang
sh	shua	shuo	shuai	shui	shuan	shun	shuang
r	rua	ruo		rui	ruan	run	
g	gua	guo	guai	gui	guan	gun	guang
k	kua	kuo	kuai	kui	kuan	kun	kuang
h	hua	huo	huai	hui	huan	hun	huang

	ü	üe	üan	ün
d				
t				
n	nü	nüe		
l	lü	lüe		
j	ju	jue	juan	jun
q	qu	que	quan	qun
x	xu	xue	xuan	xun

2. 辨音练习 (biàn yīn liànxí) Distinguish the sounds:

duo—tuo dui—tui duan—tuan dun—tun
ku—gu kuai—guai kun—gun kuang—guang
hu—hua hai—huai hei—hui han—huan
jue—que juan—quan jun—qun xie—xue
zhu—chu chu—shu zhua—shua zhui—chui
zhai—zhuai zhan—zhuan zhen—zhun
zhang—zhuang

chai—chuai　chan—chuan　chen—chun
chang—chuang
shai—shuai　shan—shuan　shen—shun
shang—shuang

二、声调练习 (shēngdiào liànxí) Get the tones right:

xuē xué xuě xuè
xiāo xiáo xiǎo xiào } xué xiào (school)

jiāo jiáo jiǎo jiào
shī shí shǐ shì } jiào shì (classroom)

shuī shuí shuǐ shuì
guō guó guǒ guò } shuǐ guǒ (fruit)

qī qí qǐ qì
chuāng chuáng chuǎng chuàng } qǐ chuáng (get up)

xī xí xǐ xì
zāo záo zǎo zào } xǐ zǎo (take a bath)

ān quán (safety)　　　bàozhǐ (newspaper)
cān guān (visit)　　　diàn huà (telephone)
fāng fǎ (method)　　　guān zhào (look after)
hé píng (peace)　　　jiě jué (solve)
kāi xué (school begins)　　lì rùn (profit)
miàn bāo (bread)　　　néng lì (ability)
péi tóng (accompany)　　qiāo mén (knock at the door)

rén mín (people)　　shuì jiào (sleep)
tóng zhì (comrade)　wǔ huì (dance party)
xiū xi (rest)　　　　yǐn liào (drinks)
zhuō zi (table)

课文
Text

A:嗨,安娜,你认识山口吗?
B:谁是山口?
A:我的日本朋友。
B:对不起,我不认识。

A:谢文,那是谁?
B:山口!
A:她是留学生吗?
B:是。我们是同学。
A:你们是朋友吗?
B:我们是好朋友!

A:嗨,山口!
B:嗨,谢文!
A:山口,我介绍一下,这是安娜!
B:你的朋友?
A:是,安娜也是我的朋友。
B:是你的女朋友吗?

A:安娜,你说呢?
C:不,我不是他的女朋友!
B:我也不是他的女朋友,哈哈哈……
C:再见!
B:再见!

汉语拼音课文
Text in *Pinyin*

A: Hāi, Annà, nǐ rènshi Shānkǒu ma?
B: Shuí shì Shānkǒu?
A: Wǒ de Rìběn péngyou.
B: Duìbuqǐ, wǒ bù rènshi.

A: Xiè Wén, nà shì shuí?
B: Shānkǒu!
A: Tā shì liúxuéshēng ma?
B: Shì. Wǒmen shì tóngxué.
A: Nǐmen shì péngyou ma?
B: Wǒmen shì hǎo péngyou!

A: Hāi, Shānkǒu!
B: Hāi, Xiè Wén!
A: Shānkǒu, wǒ jièshào yīxià, zhè shì Ānnà!
B: Nǐ de péngyou?
A: Shì, Annà yě shì wǒ de péngyou.

B：Shì nǐ de nǚ péngyou ma?
A：Ānnà, nǐ shuō ne?
C：Bù, wǒ bù shì tā de nǚ péngyou!
B：Wǒ yě bù shì tā de nǚ péngyou, hā hā hā...
C：Zàijiàn!
B：Zàijiàn!

生词
New Words

1.	的	de	(used after an attribute, indicating possession, connection or relation)
2.	朋友	péngyou	friend
3.	那	nà	that
4.	留学生	liúxuéshēng	foreign student
5.	们	men	(used after a personal pronoun or a noun to form a plural)
6.	同学	tóngxué	schoolmate, fellow student; (a form of address used in speaking to a student)
7.	介绍	jièshào	introduce; introduction
8.	一下	yīxià	in a short while; all at once; one time
9.	女	nǚ	female, woman, girl, daughter

10.	说	shuō	speak, talk, say
11.	哈	hā	Aha
12.	再见	zàijiàn	goodbye

专名
Proper Noun

山口　　　Shānkǒu　　　Yamaguchi

注释
Notes

一、元音 i 单独成音节时,要写成 yi,在一个音节开头时,要写成 y。如:

The vowel i, when it is a syllable by itself, is written as yi. When it is at the beginning of a syllable, it is written as y.

  i—yi yīdiǎn (a little), yībiān (one side)
  ie—ye yěshì (also), yèwǎn (night)
  ia—ya yáchǐ (tooth), yàjūn (runner-up)
  iao—yao yāoqǐng (invite), yàojǐn (important)

in、ing 自成音节时,要写成 yīn、yīng。如 Yīngyǔ (English)。

When in or ing stands alone as a syllable, they should be written as yin or ying respectively, e.g. Yīngyǔ.

二、元音 u 单独成音节时,要写成 wu,在一个音节的开头时,要写成 w。如:

The vowel u, when it is a syllable by itself, is written as wu. When it is at the beginning of a syllable, it is written as w.

  u—wu wūzi (room), wùhuì (misunderstand)
  uo—wo wǒmen (we, us), wòpù (sleeping berth)
  uan—wan wánxiào (joke), wǎn'ān (good night)

三、元音ü在单独成音节或在一个音节开头时,要写成yu;在ü及ü开头的韵母和声母j、q、x相拼时,ü上的两点要省去。如:

The vowel ü, when it is a syllable by itself, or when it is at the beginning of a syllable, is written as yu. When ü or other vowels beginning with ü are spelled with j, q or x, the two dots of ü should be omitted.

  ü—yu Hànyǔ (Chinese), yúkuài (joyful)
  üan—yuan yuǎnjìn (far and near), yuànyì (willing)
  jü—ju jūzhù (live), júzi (tangerine)
  qü—qu jiāoqū (suburbs), qùnián (last year)
  xü—xu xūyào (need), xǔduō (many)

四、"的",助词,用在定语和中心语之间,表示修饰或限定关系。例如:

的 is an auxiliary word placed between the attribute and the noun head to express a modifying or determining relationship.

  谁的书 我的朋友 她的老师
  谢文的同学 经理的秘书 爸爸的弟弟
  很好的朋友

五、"一下",用在动词后面,表示做一次或试着做;也表示短暂的时间。例如：

一下 is used after a verb, indicating doing something once or trying to do something. It also expresses a very short time.

说一下　谢一下
介绍一下　认识一下

补充生词
Additional New Words

男	nán	man, son, boy, male
太太	tàitai	Mrs., Madame, wife
先生	xiānsheng	teacher, Mister, husband
爱人	àiren	husband or wife, lover
同事	tóngshì	colleague
书	shū	book

练习
Exercises

一、**替换练习**：

Substitution drills:

A:<u>山口</u>,你认识<u>杰克</u>吗？
B:<u>杰克</u>是谁？
A:<u>杰克</u>是我的<u>美国</u>朋友。
B:对不起,我不认识。

安娜	谢文	法国
杰克	朱丽亚	俄罗斯
谢文	山口	日本

A:嗨,我介绍一下,这是谢文。
B:你的朋友?
A:是,谢文是我的朋友。
B:他是美国人吗?
A:不,他不是美国人。

安娜	同事	俄罗斯
朱丽亚	秘书	法国
山口	经理	日本
杰克	老师	英国

二、给下列句子标注拼音,然后朗读,注意语调:

Give the phonetic notation of the following sentences, and then read them aloud, paying special attention to the intonation:

谁? 他是谁?
你的朋友 他是我的中国朋友。
我的朋友 他是你的中国朋友?

三、把下面的词组成句子:

Unscramble the following into normal sentences:

1. 他 朋友 的 是 我
2. 我 留学生 是 美国
3. 他 杰克 认识 朋友 的
4. 介绍 你 朋友 的 一下

四、为下列单词写拼音并组句熟读:

Give the phonetic notation of the following words and then use them to make sentences and read them repeatedly:

1. 爸爸——的——学生/学生——的——爸爸
   爸爸——的——好——学生/学生——的——好——爸爸

2. 我——认识——爸爸——的——同事

爸爸——的——同事——也——认识——我

3. 爸爸——的——同事——介绍——他——的——女——朋友

他——的——女——朋友——介绍——爸爸——的——同事

模仿上面的例句,把下面的词组成句子,看谁组成的句子多,然后反复朗读:

Form sentences with the following words by imitating the examples given above. See who can make the largest number of sentences and then read them repeatedly.

同学	认识	的	爸爸	我
同事	介绍		妈妈	你
朋友	是		哥哥	他
经理			姐姐	
秘书			弟弟	
			妹妹	
			安娜	
			杰克	
			谢文	

五、会话练习:

Situational conversations:

情景:A. 两个不认识的人第一次见面

Two strangers meet for the first time.

B. 三个人第一次见面,其中两个人是互相认识的朋友

Three people meet for the first time, but two of

them are friends who already know each other.

六、写课内生词，并注拼音。
Copy the new words and give the phonetic notation.

第四课　怎么称呼
Lesson 4　How to Call a Person

学拼音 xué pīnyīn

The Phonetic Alphabet (4)

一、辨音练习（biàn yīn liànxí）Distinguish the sounds：

b—p　zhēn bàng—zhēn pàng （very good indeed—very fat indeed）

　　　bái bān—pái bān (day shift—arrange shifts)

　　　bèidòng—péitóng （passive—accompany）

　　　biànyī—piányi (plain clothes—cheap)

d—t　dāpèi—tā péi （collocation—He'll pay for it）

　　　dàijià—tài jiǎ　（price—too phoney）

　　　dānxīn—tànqīn　（worry—visit one's relatives）

　　　dǐxi—tǐxì　（ins and outs—system）

g—k　gǎi dào—kāi dào　（change its course—clear the way）
　　　gānjìng—kàn qīng　（clean—see clearly）
　　　gàojǐng—kào jìn　（give an alarm—draw near）
　　　guàiyì—kuàiyì　（strange—pleased）
j—q　dǎ jiǔ—dǎ qiú　（buy wine—play ball games）
　　　jiā jiào—qiàqiǎo　（family education—by chance）
　　　jīngjì—qīnqi　（economy—relatives）
　　　jìjié—qīnqiè　（season—kind）
z—c　zǎ zhǎo—cā zǎo　（how to find it—take a sponge bath）
　　　zāiqíng—cáiqíng　（condition of a disaster—talent）
　　　zàoyáo—cǎoyào　（start a rumor—herbal medicine）
　　　zuòguài—cuòguài　（do mischief—blame sb. wrongly）
r—n　ráotou—náo tóu　（the extra given—scratch one's head）
　　　ránliào—nán liào　（fuel—difficult to expect）
　　　réncái—nèn cài　（talented person—tender vegetables）
　　　rìqī—nì jì　（date—go into hiding）

二、声调练习（shēngdiào liànxí）Get the tones right：

　　　bàn gōng shì　（office）　bīngjilíng　（ice cream）

Jiàn lì bǎo　　(Jianlibao)　　tú shū guǎn　　(library)
zì xíng chē　　(bicycle)
nào xiào huà　　(make a fool of oneself)
niàn shēng cí　　(read the new words)
xiě Hàn zì　　(write Chinese characters)
tīng lù yīn　　(listen to recordings)
zuò liàn xí　　(do exercises)
chá yú fàn hòu　　(over a cup of tea or after a meal——at one's leisure)
Kě kǒu kě lè　　(Coca-Cola)
fù xí kè wén　　(review the texts)
yù xí shēng cí　　(preview the new words)
Hàn Yīng cídiǎn　　(Chinese-English dictionary)
Jīng mào dà xué　　(University of International Business and Economics)
shēng yì xīng lóng　　(business is booming)
cái yuán mào shèng　　(rich financial resources)

课文
Text

A:你姓什么？
B:我姓万。
A:叫什么名字？
B:文杰。万文杰！

A:请进！
B:你是高先生吗？
A:我是高亚安,您怎么称呼？
B:我姓万,叫万文杰。
A:啊,万先生,请坐！
B:谢谢！

A:请问,您贵姓？
B:免贵,姓万,万文杰。
A:啊,是万先生,幸会。
B:幸会！

汉语拼音课文
Text in *Pinyin*

A: Nǐ xìng shénme?
B: Wǒ xìng Wàn.

A: Jiào shénme míngzi?
B: Wénjié. Wàn Wénjié!

A: Qǐng jìn!
B: Nǐ shì Gāo xiānsheng ma?
A: Wǒ shì Gāo Yà'ān. Nín zěnme chēnghu?
B: Wǒ xìng Wàn, jiào Wàn Wénjié.
A: À, Wàn xiānsheng, qǐng zuò!
B: Xièxie!

A: Qǐng wèn, nín guì xìng?
B: Miǎn guì, xìng Wàn. Wàn Wénjié.
A: À, shì Wàn xiānsheng, xìnghuì!
B: Xìnghuì!

生词
New Words

1.	怎么	zěnme	how, why
2.	称呼	chēnghu	call, address
3.	姓	xìng	surname, family name
4.	什么	shénme	what
5.	叫	jiào	name, call
6.	名字	míngzi	name
7.	请	qǐng	please, request, invite
8.	进	jìn	enter, come in; into

9.	坐	zuò	sit
10.	问	wèn	ask, inquire
11.	您	nín	(honorific) you
12.	贵	guì	(honorific) your; expensive
13.	免	miǎn	dismiss, dispense with, avoid
14.	幸会	xìnghuì	very pleased to meet you

专名
Proper Nouns

高亚安	Gāo Yà'ān	Gao Ya'an
万文杰	Wàn Wénjié	Wan Wenjie

注释
Notes

一、现代汉语普通话的声调,除四个基本声调和轻声外,有些字连读时,还会出现声调变化,学习时要用心掌握和多练习。

Apart from the four basic tones and the light tone, the tones in modern Chinese also include tone variations when words are read together. This requires special attention and repeated practice.

1. 两个或几个第三声连读字,除最后一个字读原调外,前面的字都要读成二声,书写时仍标原调号。如:

When two or several characters in the third tone are read together, while the last character retains the original third tone, the others are changed into the second tone. But the original tone mark is kept in the phonetic spelling.

Nǐ hǎo → Ní hǎo
Wǒ hěn hǎo → Wó hén hǎo

2. 第三声的字在其他三个声调字和绝大部分轻声字前面时,要念成半三声,调值为(21),如:

Characters in the third tone, when occuring before characters in the other three tones or the light tone, are pronounced as the first half of the third tone, the tone pitch being (21):

Nǐ hǎo ma?
qǐng wèn
hěn máng

hǎo、qǐng、hěn 都只读前一半降调。

Hao, qing and hen in the above examples are all read as the first half of the third tone, which is actually falling.

3. "不"字单用或在第一、二、三声字前读第四声。如:

When the character 不 is used by itself, or when it is used before characters in the first, second or third tones, it is pronounced in the fourth tone.

bù gāi (shouldn't) bù néng (can't) bù hǎo (not good)
在第四声字前读第二声,书写时即直接标为第二声。如:

When it is used before characters in the fourth tone, it is pronounced in the second tone. In phonetic spelling, it is marked as the second tone in this case.

bù huì → bú huì
bù qù → bú qù
bù shì → bú shì

二、"您"和"你",都是第二人称代词。"您"是敬称,比较客气,多用来称呼长者或第一次见面的同辈。如果是很熟悉的同事或很好的朋友,用"您"称呼对方,反而显得太客气了,用"你"倒更合适一些。

你 and 您 are both second person pronouns. 您 is honorific, which is more polite, and usually used to address a senior person or someone who one meets for the first time. Between well-acquainted colleagues or good friends, 您 sounds too polite for addressing the other person. In these circumstances, 你 is more appropriate.

三、"贵姓",在询问对方姓名时,为了表示尊敬与礼貌,常说"您贵姓?"对方回答时为了表示客气,常说"免贵",甚至回答说"贱姓……"。"贵"和"贱",恰是一对反义词。询问男性的名字用"大名",询问女性的名字用"芳名",也是一种客气的询问方式。

贵姓 (honorable surname)

To show respect and politeness, "您贵姓?" is often used to ask the other person's name. In reply, the other person would say:免贵… or even 贱姓…. 贵 and 贱 are a pair of antonyms. Also for the sake of politeness, 大名 (big name) is used to ask a male's name, while 芳名 (sweet name) is used to ask a lady's name.

补充生词
Additional New Words

贱	jiàn	humble, low-priced
芳名	fāngmíng	the name of a young woman
大名	dàmíng	(honorific) your name; one's formal personal name
久仰	jiǔyǎng	I have heard about you for a long time.

练习
Exercises

一、替换练习：
Substitution drills：

A：你姓什么？
B：我姓<u>关</u>。
A：你叫什么名字？
B：我叫<u>关　　　</u>。

朱	朱同文
安	安小朋
谢	谢贵友

A：请问，您贵姓？
B：我姓<u>安</u>。
A：怎么称呼？
B：我的中国名字叫<u>安小朋</u>。
A：你是留学生吗？
B：是。我是<u>法国</u>留学生。

谢	谢贵友	俄罗斯
朱	朱丽亚	美国
韩	韩绍芳	英国

45

A：请问，你的<u>经理</u>是谁？
B：他姓<u>万</u>，叫<u>万文杰</u>。
A：<u>万文杰</u>？我认识他。
B：你认识我的<u>经理</u>，我很高兴。

| 秘书 | 朱 | 朱丽亚 |
| 老师 | 高 | 高文英 |

二、把下面的词组成句子：

Unscramble the following into normal sentences：

1. 他　什么　名字　叫

2. 你　经理　称呼　怎么　的

3. 你　芳名　的　久仰

4. 名字　你是　谢贵友　吗　的　叫

三、完成对话：

Complete the following dialogues：

A：你是万先生吗？
B：_____，_____。您怎么称呼？
A：_____。
B：很高兴认识你。
A：_____。

A：请问，您贵姓？
B：_____，_____。
A：久仰，久仰。
B：你是……
A：我是_____。

B:幸会,幸会。

四、用下列动词短语各组两个句子:

Use each of the following verbal groups to form two sentences:

例:你去请一下老师。

1. 介绍一下

2. 问一下

3. 认识一下

五、会话练习:

Situational Conversations:

情景1:你去拜访一位你还不认识的人。

You go and visit someone you don't know.

情景2:两个不认识的人初次见面,彼此问候并询问对方情况。

Two strangers meet for the first time, greeting and inquiring about each other.

六、写课内生词,并注拼音。

Copy the new words and give the phonetic notation.

第五课 打电话
Lesson 5 Making Telephone Calls

课文
Text

A：喂，你好！这是54972143。
B：你好！请问，谢太太在吗？
A：你的电话错了！
B：对不起！

A：喂，你好！这是爱友公司。
B：你好！请问，高亚安先生在吗？
A：他不在。你有什么事吗？
B：啊，请他给我打电话。
A：你的电话号码是……
B：68370641。
A：好的，再见！

A：喂，是68370641吗？
B：是，我是万文杰。

A:我是高亚安。
B:我给你打电话,你不在。
A:你有什么事吗?
B:你知道谢太太的电话吗?
A:知道,64960057。
B:好,谢谢!

汉语拼音课文
Text in *Pinyin*

A: Wèi, nǐ hǎo! Zhè shì 54972143.
B: Nǐ hǎo! Qǐng wèn, Xiè tàitai zài ma?
A: Nǐ de diànhuà cuò le!
B: Duìbuqǐ!

A: Wèi, nǐ hǎo! Zhè shì Àiyǒu gōngsī.
B: Nǐ hǎo! Qǐng wèn, Gāo Yà'ān xiānsheng zài ma?
A: Tā bù zài. Nǐ yǒu shénme shì ma?
B: À, qǐng tā gěi wǒ dǎ diànhuà.
A: Nǐ de diànhuà hàomǎ shì ...
B: 68370641.
A: Hǎo de, zàijiàn!

A: Wèi, shì 68370641 ma?
B: Shì, wǒ shì Wàn Wénjié.
A: Wǒ shì Gāo Yà'ān.

B：Wǒ gěi nǐ dǎ diànhuà, nǐ bù zài.
A：Nǐ yǒu shénme shì ma?
B：Nǐ zhīdao Xiè tàitai de diànhuà ma?
A：Zhīdao, 64960057.
B：Hǎo, xièxie!

生词
New Words

1.	打	dǎ	make (a call), strike, play
2.	电话	diànhuà	telephone
3.	在	zài	(preposition indicating time, place, situation or scope)
4.	错	cuò	wrong; fault
5.	公司	gōngsī	company, corporation
6.	有	yǒu	have, possess; there be
7.	事	shì	thing, matter, affair
8.	给	gěi	give
9.	号码	hàomǎ	number
10.	知道	zhīdào	know, realize, be aware of
11.	一(1)	yī	one
12.	二(2)	èr	two
13.	三(3)	sān	three
14.	四(4)	sì	four
15.	五(5)	wǔ	five
16.	六(6)	liù	six

17. 七(7)	qī	seven
18. 八(8)	bā	eight
19. 九(9)	jiǔ	nine
20. 十(10)	shí	ten
21. 零(0)	líng	zero
22. 喂	wèi	hello, hey

注释
Notes

一、"在",动词,表示人或事物的存在,后边跟的宾语是存在的处所、位置。"在"的宾语常省略。否定形式是在动词"在"的前面加副词"不"。例如:

在, verb, expresses the existence of a person or thing. The object that follows it indicates the place or location of the existence. Its object is often omitted. The negative form is to add the adverb 不 before the verb 在.

A:高先生在吗?
B:高先生不在。

A:高先生在家吗?
B:他不在家。

1. 经理办公室在315。
2. 他的宿舍在407。

二、"给",介词。介词不能单独使用,它后面必须跟名词、代词或词

组构成介词结构,一起在句子中充当定语、状语、补语。例如:

给 is used as a preposition, which cannot be used alone. It is followed by a noun, a pronoun or a phrase to form a prepositional structure to function as attribute, adverbial or complement in a sentence.

1. 请给我打电话!
2. 给我介绍一下。

三、现代汉语的句子成分:汉语的句子,一般都有主语、谓语、宾语三个基本成分和附加修饰成分。主语和宾语前面可以有定语。定语是修饰和限定主语和宾语的。谓语前面可以有状语,状语表示谓语的情态、程度、范围、时间、处所等;谓语后面可以有补语,补充说明谓语的结果、程度、时间、处所、数量等。汉语句子成分的排列顺序如下:

(定语)主语 → 〔状语〕谓语〈补语〉→ (定语)宾语

符号表示:

主══ 谓—— 宾～～ 定( ) 状〔 〕
补〈 〉

Elements of sentence structure in modern Chinese:

A Chinese sentence generally contains three basic elements (subject, predicate, and object), and other supplementary modifying elements.

Preceding the subject or the object, there may be the attributive, which is to modify or determine the subject or the object. Preceding the predicate there can be the adverbial, which tells the manner, degree, scope, time, or place of the predicate. Following the predicate there can be the complement, which explains the result, degree, time, place, or quantity of the predicate. The sequence of the elements of Chinese sentence structure can be shown in the following diagram:

(attributive) subject → (adverbial) predicate (complement) → (attributive) object

They can also be indicated by the following signs:

Subject: ＝＝　　　Attributive: ( )
Predicate: ——　　Adverbial: 〔 〕
Object: ～～　　　Complement: 〈 〉

例如:

1. 我 叫 杰克。
2. 我 认识 (他的) 老师。
3. (他的) 妹妹 是 (我的) 朋友。
4. 我们 认识 〈一下〉。
5. 我 〔很 高兴〕 认识 (你的) 同事。

补充生词

Additional New Words

转	zhuǎn	pass on, transfer, turn
占线	zhànxiàn	engaged
办公室	bàngōngshì	office
宿舍	sùshè	dormitory, hostel
教室	jiàoshì	classroom
手机	shǒujī	mobile phone
呼	hū	bleep, page, call, exhale
寻呼台	xúnhūtái	paging station
留言	liúyán	leave a message

练习
Exercises

一、**替换练习**：

Substitution drills：

A：你好！请问<u>山口小姐</u>在吗？
B：她不在，你是谁？
A：对不起，我是她的朋友，叫<u>高亚安</u>。
B：请问，你有什么事吗？
A：请她给我打电话。
B：好的。

万经理	杰克
安秘书	朱丽亚
朱老师	谢文

A：喂，请问，<u>高亚安</u>在吗？
B：<u>高亚安</u>，你的电话！
A：<u>高亚安</u>吗，我是<u>谢文</u>。
C：你好，<u>谢文</u>，有什么事吗？
A：你知道<u>山口办公室</u>的电话吗？
C：知道。<u>6 4 9 4 7 3 6 2</u>。
A：好，谢谢。

安娜	朱丽亚	杰克	宿舍	64938754
万文杰	安娜	老师	教室	64967235
杰克	安亚娜	万经理	公司	68479601

二、**把下面的词组成句子**：

Unscramble the following into normal sentences：

1. 你 谁 电话 给 打

54

2. 我　不　电话　她　号码　知道　的

3. 你　电话　请问　的　号码

4. 打　你　了　错　电话

5. 请　办公室　我　电话　给　打

三、完成对话：
Complete the following dialogues：

A：你知道山口宿舍的电话号码吗？
B：_____，_____。

A：请问，万经理在吗？
B：_____，_____。

A：安小姐不在吗？请她给我打电话。
B：_____。

A：经理不在，您有什么事吗？
B：_____。

四、根据下面数字山读出各种组合，练习自己的发音：
Practice pronunciation by forming combinations of the figures given in the following triangle：

55

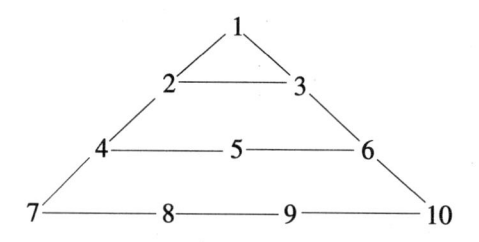

五、换词组句练习(三句以上):

Replace the underlined words in the following to make new sentences:

1. 请<u>你</u>给<u>我</u>打电话。

2. 你<u>有</u>什么事吗?

六、把下面的词或词组扩展成句子:

Expand the following words or expressions into sentences:

1. 电话 2. 事
   打电话   什么事
   请打电话   有什么事

3. 号码
   电话号码
   你的电话号码

七、会话练习:

Situational Conversations:

情景 1：A 给 B 打电话，开始电话没人接，后来电话占线，最后电话通了。

　　A is calling B. At first, nobody answers, then the line is engaged. Finally he gets through.

情景 2：B 给 A 打电话，A 不在办公室，B 给 A 的 BP 机留言。

　　B is calling A. A is not in the office. B leaves a message for A's bleeper.

八、阅读《普通话声韵拼合总表》。

　　Read the *Table of the Combinations of the Initials and Finals in Common Speech*.

第六课　预订房间
Lesson 6　Booking a Room

课文
Text

A:您好！这是北京饭店服务台。
B:我要预订一个房间。
A:要套间吗？
B:不！标准间。
A:什么时候来？
B:明天。
A:请问先生贵姓？
B:我姓王。
A:恭候您的光临！

A:小姐,我要一个房间。
B:预订了吗？
A:昨天我打电话预订了。
B:请问先生贵姓？
A:我姓王。

B:请等等。3702房间,可以吗?

A:可以,谢谢!

B:别客气!

汉语拼音课文
Text in *Pinyin*

A: Nínhǎo! Zhè shì Běijīng Fàndiàn fúwùtái.

B: Wǒ yào yùdìng yī gè fángjiān.

A: Yào tàojiān ma?

B: Bù! Biāozhǔn jiān.

A: Shénme shíhou lái?

B: Míngtiān.

A: Qǐngwèn xiānsheng guì xìng?

B: Wǒ xìng Wáng.

A: Gōnghòu nín de guānglín!

A: Xiǎojie, wǒ yào yī gè fángjiān.

B: yùdìng le ma?

A: Zuótiān wǒ dǎ diànhuà yùdìng le.

B: Qǐngwèn xiānsheng guì xìng?

A: Wǒ xìng Wáng.

B: Qǐng děngdeng. 3702 fángjiān, kěyǐ ma?

A: Kěyǐ, xièxie!

B: Bié kèqi!

生词
New Words

1.	预订	yùdìng	book, subscribe; reservation
2.	服务台	fúwùtái	service desk, reception desk
3.	要	yào	want, ask for
4.	个	gè	(a general measure word)
5.	房间	fángjiān	room
6.	标准间	biāozhǔn jiān	standard room
7.	套间	tàojiān	suite
8.	时候	shíhou	time, moment
9.	来	lái	come
10.	明天	míngtiān	tomorrow
11.	王	Wáng	Wang (a surname)
12.	恭候	gōnghòu	await respectfully
13.	光临	guānglín	honor sb. with one's presence
14.	了	le	(auxiliary word indicating the completion of an action)
15.	昨天	zuótiān	yesterday
16.	等	děng	wait, await
17.	可以	kěyǐ	can, may
18.	别	bié	don't, had better not
19.	客气	kèqi	polite, courteous

专名
Proper Noun

北京饭店　Běijīng Fàndiàn　　　Beijing Hotel

注释
Notes

一、"个",量词。汉语里有大量量词,能够计量的人或事物,都有特定的量词,这是在长期的社会交际活动中形成的,是一种"习惯用法",不可乱用。量词的使用,是外国朋友学习中的一个难点,学习时要特别注意。下面是量词"个"的常用例子:

个 is a measure word. There are many measure words in Chinese. Each of the persons or things to be measured goes with a specific measure word. These have resulted from the long years of social communications and become set expressions which cannot be changed randomly. The use of measure words is a difficult area for foreign friends to learn Chinese and merits special attention in their studies. What follows are some common examples of the use of the measure word 个:

一个人	三个宿舍
一个教师	四个弟弟
一个教室	一个晚上
一个房间	十个学生

二、"了",助词,附在动词后边,表示动作已经完成。例如:

了, an auxiliary word, is used after a verb to indicate that

the action has been completed.

> 他来了。
> 他预订了一个房间。
> 杰克今天换了钱。
> 我刚才给她打了电话。

三、"恭候光临",是一句礼貌语,意思是"恭敬地等候您的到来"、"您的到来,是我们的光荣",常用在正式的请柬上。现在,商场、饭店在欢迎顾客时,也常用这句话。

恭候光临 is a polite expression which means "await your presence respectfully" or "it is our honor to have your company". It is often used in a formal invitation. Now it is also often used by stores, hotels and restaurants in welcoming their guests.

补充生词
Additional New Words

今天	jīntiān	today
前天	qiántiān	the day before yesterday
后天	hòutiān	the day after tomorrow
单人间	dānrén jiān	single room
双人间	shuāngrén jiān	double room

练习
Exercises

一、替换练习：
Substitution drills：

A:小姐,可以预订房间吗?
B:可以。请问先生贵姓?
A:我姓谢。
B:先生要什么房间?
A:一个单人间。

万	双人间
朱	套间
安	标准间

A:小姐,我要一个房间。
B:你预订了吗?
A:我昨天预订了。
B:先生贵姓?
A:我姓谢。
B:请等等。7023号房间,可以吗?
A:可以。

前天	万	1409
昨天下午	安	5678
今天上午	朱	3642

A:先生,这是您的房间。
B:啊,不错。
A:有什么事,请打电话。
　服务台的电话是0109
B:谢谢!
A:别客气!

| 小姐 | 很好 | 4001 |
| 夫人 | 太好了 | 2323 |

二、把下面的词组成句子：

63

Unscramble the following into normal sentences:

1. 饭店　吗　服务台　是

2. 王秘书　我　预订　给　房间　一个

3. 你　打　预订　可以　电话　房间

4. 先生　时候　饭店　来　什么

三、完成对话：

Complete the following dialogues:

A：请问，可以预订房间吗？
B：_____。
A：你预订的房间好吗？
B：_____。
A：在你的房间可以打电话吗？
B：_____。
A：北京饭店的服务好吗？
B：_____。

四、组词练习：

Word formation：

打____　　知道____　　认识____
问____　　介绍____　　预订____
____
____ 台

五、扩展句子,然后熟读:

Expand the following into sentences, and then read them repeatedly:

1. 房间
   单人房间
   一个单人房间

2. 等
   等你
   等你来

六、会话练习:

Situational conversations:

情景:打电话预订房间(标准间,单人间,双人间,套间)。
Book a room by phone (a standard room, a single room, a double room, a suite).

七、给下面的拼音标上调号,然后朗读几遍:

Mark the tones of the following and then read the passage for several times:

Wang xiansheng gei Beijing Fandian da dianhua, ta shuo, ta yao yuding yi ge fangjian, shi yi ge biaozhun jian. Beijing Fandian fuwu tai de xiaojie wen ta: "Shenme shihou lai fandian?" Wang xiansheng shuo: "Mingtian." Fuwu tai de xiaojie shuo: "Gonghou nin de guanglin!"

第七课　换钱
Lesson 7　Changing Money

课文
Text

A:小姐,我们要换钱。
B:是现金还是旅行支票?
A:是现金。
C:我的是旅行支票。
B:你们要换多少?
A:今天银行的汇率是多少?
B:100美元兑换823.90元人民币。
A:好的,我换500美元。你换不换?
C:我不换了。
A:小姐,我刚才换了500美元的人民币。
B:有什么问题吗?
A:今天100美元兑换823.90元人民币,对吗?
B:对!
A:500美元换4219.50元?
B:先生,是4119.50元,不是4219.50元。

A:哦,是我算错了,对不起!
B:没关系!

汉语拼音课文
Text in *Pinyin*

A: Xiǎojie, wǒmen yào huàn qián.
B: Shì xiànjīn háishì lǚxíng zhīpiào?
A: Shì xiànjīn.
C: Wǒde shì lǚxíng zhīpiào.
B: Nǐmen yào huàn duōshao?
A: Jīntiān yínháng de huìlǜ shì duōshao?
B: Yī bǎi Měiyuán duìhuàn bā bǎi èrshísān kuài jiǔ máo Rénmínbì.
A: Hǎo de, wǒ huàn wǔ bǎi Měiyuán. Nǐ huàn bù huàn?
C: Wǒ bù huàn le.
A: Xiǎojie, wǒ gāngcái huàn le wǔ bǎi Měiyuán de Rénmínbì.
B: Yǒu shénme wèntí ma?
A: Jīntiān yī bǎi Měiyuán duìhuàn bā bǎi èrshísān kuài jiǔ máo Rénmínbì, duì ma?
B: Duì!
A: Wǔ bǎi Měiyuán huàn sì qiān èr bǎi yīshíjiǔ kuài wǔ máo?
B: Xiānsheng, shì sì qiān yī bǎi yīshíjiǔ kuài wǔ máo,

bù shì sì qiān èr bǎi yīshíjiǔ kuài wǔ máo.
A：O, shì wǒ suàn cuò le, duìbuqǐ!
B：Méi guānxi!

生词
New Words

1. 换　　　huàn　　　　　change, exchange
2. 钱　　　qián　　　　　money
3. 银行　　yínháng　　　bank
4. 块　　　kuài　　　　　yuan, dollar; piece, lump
5. 现金　　xiànjīn　　　cash
6. 还是　　háishì　　　　or; still, yet
7. 旅行　　lǚxíng　　　　travel, tour, journey
8. 支票　　zhīpiào　　　cheque
9. 多少　　duōshao　　　how many, how much
10. 汇率　　huìlǜ　　　　exchange rate
11. 兑换　　duìhuàn　　　exchange, convert
12. 元(块)　yuán(kuài)　yuan (kuai)
13. 刚才　　gāngcái　　　a moment ago; just now
14. 问题　　wèntí　　　　question, problem, issue
15. 算　　　suàn　　　　　calculate, compute, figure
16. 哦　　　ò　　　　　　oh

专名
Proper Nouns

美元	Měiyuán	U. S. dollar
人民币	Rénmínbì	Renminbi

注释
Notes

一、"要",动词,表示希望得到或保持什么。例如：
要, as a verb, expresses that one wants something or wants to keep something.

> 我要一本书。
> 我要三元钱。
> 他要标准间。
> 他要你的电话号码。

"要",也是助动词,放在动词或形容词前,表示可能、必要或愿望等,否定形式一般是在助动词前加否定副词"不"。例如：
要 is also an auxiliary verb, used before a verb or an adjective to express a possibility, necessity or wish. The negative form is generally to add the negative adverb 不 before the auxiliary verb.

> 她不要换钱。
> 经理要预订一个房间。
> 我要好好谢谢老师。

二、"换不换？"这是一种正反疑问句。正反疑问句,是用谓语的肯定＋否定形式表示疑问,即"谓语＋不(没)＋谓语"。这种疑问句,要作出肯定或否定的明确回答。例如：

换不换？ This is called a positive and negative question. It is formed by the positive form of the predicate ＋ the negative form of the predicate, i.e., predicate ＋ 不(or 没) ＋ predicate. This kind of question requires a definite positive or negative answer.

A:你认识不认识安娜？
B:我认识。

A:你们经理好不好？
B:不好！

A:他高兴不高兴？
B:他很不高兴！

三、"还是",连词,用在选择疑问句中。选择疑问句,是句子中并列出两项或多项情况,要求选择其中一项回答。例如：

还是, as a conjunction, is used in an alternative question, which is to select from two or more alternatives listed in the sentence.

A:你兑换还是不兑换？
B:我不兑换了！

A:你今天晚上来还是不来？
B:我今天晚上不来了。

A:你要单人间还是双人间？
B:我要双人间。

补充生词
Additional New Words

比价	bǐjià	rate of exchange, price relations
角(毛)	jiǎo (máo)	1/10 of a yuan
分	fēn	1/100 of a yuan
百(100)	bǎi (yī bǎi)	hundred
千(1000)	qiān (yī qiān)	thousand
万(10000)	wàn (yī wàn)	ten thousand
点	diǎn	point, dot, drop
英镑	Yīngbàng	pound sterling
法朗	Fǎláng	franc
日元	Rìyuán	Japanese yen
马克	Mǎkè	mark
香港元	Xiānggǎng Yuán	Hong Kong dollar

练习
Exercises

一、**替换练习**:

Substitution drills:

A: 你有钱吗?
B: 有。
A: 有多少?
B: 有38元。

50 元	100 元
120 元	290 元
336 元	

A:小姐,我换钱。
B:现金还是旅行支票?
A:现金。

美元	英镑
日元	法朗
美元	日元

A:小姐,今天银行的汇率是多少?
B:你是问美元兑换人民币的比价吗?
A:是的。
B:100美元兑换823.90元人民币。

日元	6.572元
英镑	1364.6元
港元	107.12元

二、完成对话:

Complete the following dialogues:

A:小姐,我要换钱。
B:_____?

A:你是美国人还是英国人?
B:我是_____。

A:_____还是_____?
B:我是中国学生。

A:你今天换不换钱?
B:不,_____。

A:你有什么事?
B:我要_____。

三、给下面的词语配上适当的动词,然后扩展成句子:

First add a verb to each of the following, and then expand them into sentences:

____朋友　　____钱　　____房间　　____电话

四、完成句子：

Complete the following sentences:

1. _____介绍还是不介绍_____。

2. _____等还是不等_____。

3. _____要换钱还是不要换钱。

4. ____要预订还是不要预订_____。

五、将下列正反疑问句改成一般问句，然后作出回答：

Turn the following positive and negative questions into general questions and then answer them:

例：你打不打电话？
　　你打电话吗？

1. 你等不等你的朋友？

2. 先生预订不预订房间？

3. 他要不要现金？

4. 你换不换钱？

5. 今天晚上经理问不问他的秘书？

六、快速读出下面的数：

Read the following figures quickly：

1.50 元	1 元 2 角 3 分	643 元人民币
1.23 元	3 元 5 角 8 分	18456 元人民币
4.10 元	10 元 4 角 5 分	197274 元人民币
11.37 元	21 元零 8 分	

七、会话练习：

Situational conversation：

情景：一个美国留学生在银行服务台换钱

An American student is changing money at the counter of a bank.

八、阅读下面的一段话，然后用拼音把这段话写出来：

Read the following passage, and then put it into phonetic notation：

今天，一个留学生在银行换钱。他换了钱，算了算，"啊，不对，银行少给了我一百元钱。""小姐，你少给了我一百元钱！"小姐说："您刚才换了五百美元，我给了您四千一百一十九元五角，您再算算！"他说："啊，是我算错了，对不起！"

第八课　出租车
Lesson 8　Taxi

课文
Text

A:出租车!
B:先生,请上车!去哪儿?
A:去北京饭店。
B:请坐好!
A:到友谊商店的时候,请停一下车。
B:好的。

A:先生是来旅行吗?
B:不。我是来做生意的。
A:您刚到北京吧?
B:是。你怎么知道?
A:我是出租车司机!
B:到友谊商店了?
A:不,堵车了!
B:嗷!

75

A:先生,北京饭店到了。

B:多少钱?

A:48.50 元。

B:48.50 元? 你没有多收费吧?

A:先生,您看,这是我的车号!

B:64029。好吧,这是 50 元。

A:找您 1.50 元。

B:开张发票吧!

A:好的。

B:谢谢!

A:再见!

汉语拼音课文

Text in *Pinyin*

A：Chūzu chē!

B：xiānsheng, qǐng shàngchē! Qù nǎr?

A：Qù Běijīng Fàndiàn.

B：Qǐng zuò hǎo!

A：Dào Yòuyì Shāngdiàn de shíhou, qǐng tíng yīxià chē.

B：Hǎo de.

A：Xiānsheng shì lái lǚxíng ma?

B：Bù. Wǒ shì lái zuò shēngyi de.

A：Nín gāng dào Běijīng ba?

B：Shì. Nǐ zěnme zhīdao?
A：Wǒ shì chūzū chē sījī!
B：Dào Yǒuyì Shāngdiàn le?
A：Bù, dǔ chē le!
B：Ōu!

A：Xiānsheng, Běijīng Fàndiàn dào le.
B：Duōshao qián?
A：Sìshíbā kuài wǔ máo.
B：Sìshíbā kuài wǔ máo? Nǐ méiyǒu duō shōu fèi ba?
A：Xiānsheng, nín kàn, zhè shì wǒ de chē hào!
B：64029. Hǎo ba, zhè shì wǔshí kuài.
A：Zhǎo nín yī kuài wǔ máo.
B：Kāi zhāng fāpiào ba!
A：Hǎo de.
B：Xièxie!
A：Zàijiàn!

生词
New Words

1.	出租车	chūzū chē	taxi
2.	上车	shàng chē	get on
3.	去	qù	go
4.	哪儿	nǎr	where
5.	到	dào	arrive, reach

6.	停车	tíngchē	stop, pull up, park
7.	做	zuò	do, make, carry on
8.	生意	shēngyi	business, trade
9.	刚	gāng	just, exactly
10.	司机	sījī	driver
11.	堵车	dǔchē	traffic jam
12.	噢	ōu	oh
13.	没有	méiyǒu	not have; did not; without
14.	收费	shōufèi	collect fees, charge
15.	吧	ba	(auxiliary word used at the end of a sentence, indicating mood)
16.	看	kàn	look, see, watch
17.	找	zhǎo	give change; look for
18.	开	kāi	open, operate, write out
19.	张	zhāng	(a measure word); sheet
20.	发票	fāpiào	receipt

专名

Proper Noun

友谊商店　　Yǒuyì Shāngdiàn　　Friendship Store

注释
Notes

一、"是……的",这是一个常用句式。"的"和它前面的词或词组合成一个"的"字结构,相当于一个名词,用来表示人或事物。所指的事物,常可以省去,但从上下文中可以明白所指的是什么。例如:

是…的 is a frequently used sentence pattern. 的, together with the word or phrase that precedes it, forms a 的-structure which functions like a noun, used to indicate a person or thing. The thing being referred to can often be omitted. But one can easily know what is being referred to from the context.

  A:这是谁的书?
  B:我的(书)。

  A:这是你的车吗?
  B:不,这是他的(车)。

这个句式里的"是",是谓语。有时候,"是"还表示明显的强调语气。这时,"是"字要重读。例如:

是 in this structure is the predicate, and sometimes it carries with it a lot of emphasis. Under such circumstances, 是 should be stressed.

  A:这是你的吗? 你没有认错?
  B:没错,这是我的!

二、"刚"、"刚才",表示行为、事件等在说话前不久发生。"刚才"更强调行为或事件发生在极短的时间以前。试比较下面的句子:

刚 or 刚才 is used to indicate that a certain action or thing took place not long before the statement. 刚才 lays more emphasis on the fact that the action or event happened just a very short time before.

  1. 他刚认识安娜。
  2. 朱丽亚刚来中国。
  3. 他刚才在这儿。
  4. 他刚才去银行了。

三、"吧",语气助词。常用在句子末尾。

吧 is an auxiliary word indicating the mood. It is usually placed at the end of the sentence.

1. 表示命令、请求、催促、建议等：

It can be used to indicate a command, a request, an urging, or a suggestion：

  1）开张发票吧!
  2）你去吧!
  3）请他明天来吧!

2. 表示疑问。这种句子,常表示一种估计、推测的语气。

It can express interrogation, often with a sense of estimation or guessing：

  1）你刚到北京吧?
  2）你不认识他吧?
  3）那是王老师吧?

3. 表示同意。

It can also be used to express agreement：

  1）好吧!
  2）可以吧!

3）请来吧！

补充生词
Additional New Words

打的	dǎdī	take a taxi
公里	gōnglǐ	kilometer
起价	qǐjià	minimum charge
下车	xià chē	get off
系	jì	tie, fasten
安全带	ānquándài	safety belt
国际邮局	guójì yóujú	international post office

练习
Exercises

一、**替换练习**：

Substitution drills：

A：先生，你去哪儿？
B：我去<u>友谊商店</u>。

商店	银行
邮局	服务台
办公室	

A：小姐是来<u>留学</u>的吗？
B：不，我是来<u>旅行</u>的。

学习汉语	做生意
旅行	学习
预订房间	要出租车
找经理	找秘书

A:这是你的车吗?
B:不,这是饭店的。

房间	安娜
钱	我爸
办公室	经理
司机	杰克

二、把下面的词组成句子:

Unscramble the following into normal sentences:

1. 我　国际邮局　去　要

2. 哪儿　车　可以　停

3. 请　叫　我　给　出租车

4. 你　打的　北京饭店　可以　去

三、完成对话:

Complete the following dialogues:

A:你在中国知道怎么打的吗?
B:_____。

A:你要出租车司机开发票吗?
B:_____。

A:你来北京做什么?
B:_____。

A:北京的出租车司机多收费吗?

B：_____。

A：在北京开车,要系安全带吗？
B：_____。

四、为下列词语配上合适的动词：
Add appropriate verbs to the following：

____发票　　____生意　　____车号
____钱　　　____旅行　　____安全带　____收费
____
____车
____
____

五、为下列句子选用"刚"、"刚才",并把它放在合适的位置：
Add 刚 or 刚才 to the following sentences and get its position right：

1. 经理开车去。　　　5. 堵车了。

2. 你去哪儿了？　　　6. 他做生意。

3. 他看我的车号了。　7. 我的男朋友认识我的父亲。

4. 秘书预订房间。　　8. 司机去银行了。

六、细心体会下列句子中的"是",哪些要重读,哪些不要重读：
Which of the word 是 in the following should be stressed,

and which should not be stressed?

1. 我是开车的。　　　5. 司机是没有多收费。

2. 钱是我给的。　　　6. 你是没错,这是他的错。

3. 他是我介绍的。　　7. 你是美国人还是英国人?

4. 你这是去哪儿?　　8. 他刚才是在办公室!

七、会话练习:
Situational conversation:

情景:经理太太要去银行换钱,叫出租车。到银行,司机停下车等她换钱,太太去饭店看朋友。

The wife of the manager is going to change money at the bank. She calls a taxi and gets to the bank. The driver waits for her while she is changing money. Then she goes to a hotel to see her friend.

八、给下面的拼音标上调号,然后朗读几遍:
Mark the tones of the following and then read the passage for several times:

Yi ge Meiguo ren gang dao Beijing, zuo chuzu che qu Beijing Fandian. Ta yao chuzu che siji dao Youyi Shangdian de shihou ting yixia che. Che ting le, ta wen: "Dao Youyi Shangdian le?" Siji shuo: "Bu, du che le!" "Ou, zao tou le!" (It's too bad!)

第九课　他没来上班
Lesson 9　He Has Not Turned Up for Work

课文
Text

A:小王,给我准备车。
B:什么时候要？
A:半个小时以后。
B:好的。

A:喂,张师傅在吗？
B:他不在。
A:他去哪儿了？
B:他没来上班。
A:哦,谢谢！

A:你好！这是饭店总服务台。
B:你好！我是爱友公司。我们要一辆车。
A:什么时候用？

B：九点四十五分。
A：就是一刻钟以后,对吧？
B：对！行吗？
A：没问题。
B：谢谢！

A：经理,车已经安排好了。
B：谢谢！
A：一刻钟以后在饭店门口上车。
B：是张师傅开车吗？
A：不。张师傅今天没上班,是饭店的车。
B：好,知道了。

汉语拼音课文
Text in *Pinyin*

A：Xiǎo Wáng, gěi wǒ zhǔnbèi chē.
B：Shénme shíhou yào?
A：Bàn ge xiǎoshí yǐhòu.
B：Hǎo de.

A：Wèi, Zhāng shīfu zài ma?
B：Tā bù zài.
A：Tā qù nǎr le?
B：Tā méi lái shàngbān.
A：Ò, xièxie!

A: Nǐ hǎo! Zhè shì fàndiàn zǒng fúwùtái.
B: Nǐ hǎo! Wǒ shì Àiyǒu gōngsī. Wǒmen yào yī liàng chē.
A: Shénme shíhou yòng?
B: Jiǔ diǎn sìshíwǔ fēn.
A: Jiùshì yī kè zhōng yǐhòu, duì ba?
B: Duì! Xíng ma?
A: Méi wèntí.
B: Xièxie!

A: Jīnglǐ, chē yǐjīng ānpái hǎo le.
B: Xièxie!
A: Yī kè zhōng yǐhòu zài fàndiàn ménkǒu shàngchē.
B: Shì Zhāng shīfu kāichē ma?
A: Bù. Zhāng shīfu jīntiān méi shàngbān, shì fàndiàn de chē.
B: Hǎo, zhīdao le.

生词
New Words

1. 上班　　shàngbān　　go to work, be on duty
2. 准备　　zhǔnbèi　　prepare, get ready
3. 半　　　bàn　　　　half
4. 小时　　xiǎoshí　　hour

5.	以后	yǐhòu	after, afterwards, later
6.	师傅	shīfu	master
7.	总	zǒng	general, overall, total
8.	辆	liàng	(measure word for vehicles)
9.	用	yòng	use, employ
10.	点	diǎn	point; o'clock
11.	分	fēn	minute
12.	就是	jiùshì	exactly, precisely
13.	刻	kè	quarter (of an hour)
14.	钟	zhōng	bell, dock; (time as measured in hours and minutes)
15.	行	xíng	be all right; will do
16.	已经	yǐjīng	already
17.	安排	ānpái	arrange
18.	门口	ménkǒu	entrance, doorway, gate
19.	开车	kāichē	drive

注释
Notes

一、"不"、"没有",都是副词,表示否定。"没有"用于对动作完成的否定或对事物性质变化的否定,后面不能带"了",所以不能用于将来时间。试比较"不"和"没有"的用法。

Both 不 and 没有 are adverbs indicating negation. 没有 is used to negate the completion of an action or the change of the nature of a certain object. So it cannot take 了 after it, nor can it be used with a future time. Compare the usage between 不 and

没有.

1. 他今天不来了。(这是回答"他今天来不来?")
2. 他今天没有来。(这是回答"他今天来没来?")

3. 他昨天来了吗?
4. 他昨天也没来。(不能回答"他昨天也不来。")

5. 他明天来吗?
6. 他明天也不来。(不能回答"他明天也没来。")

"没"、"没有",也是动词。"有"表示领有、占有。"没有"是"有"的否定词。例如:

没 and 没有 can be used as verb too. 有 means possessing or owning. 没有 is the negation of 有.

1. 他有钱。
2. 我没有钱。

3. 他有秘书。
4. 我没有秘书。

二、"就是",副词,指出某种确定的范围、对象,排斥其它。例如:
就是, as an adverb, indicates a certain scope or object, excluding others.

1. 他就是今天没有来上班。(只有今天没有来上班)
2. 我们老板就是喜欢旅行。(老板不喜欢别的活动)

三、"已经",副,表示动作完成或达到了某种程度。单音节动词后

必须带"了"。形容词后,也要带"了"或"下来、起来、过来"等词。例如:

已经, adverb, expresses that an action has already finished or has reached a certain extent. In these sentences, monosyllabic verbs must be followed by 了. Adjectives are also followed by 了 or words like 下来, 起来, or 过来, etc.

1. 他已经大了。
2. 车已经停了。
3. 我们已经认识了。
4. 她已经下班了。
5. 现在已经九点了。

补充生词
Additional New Words

下班	xiàbān	get off work
过	guò	exceed; beyond, past
差	chà	be less than, be short of
整	zhěng	full, entire; exactly
现在	xiànzài	now, present

练习
Exercises

一、替换练习:
　　Substitution drills:

A:现在几点了?
B:现在八点了。

7:40	8:15
9:30	9:45
10:10	11:55
12:05	24:00

A:你们几点上班?
B:我们八点上班。

下班	下午 6:00
上课	上午 10:10
下课	11:45

二、把下面的词组成句子:

Unscramble the following into normal sentences:

1. 经理 已经 好 车 准备 了 的

2. 我们 哪儿 在 上车

3. 请 9:45 饭店 在 上车 门口

4. 今天 谁 是 开车

5. 饭店 车 没有 了 已经

三、完成对话:

Complete the following dialogues:

A:你什么时候上班,什么时候下班?
B:_____。

A:现在你有事吗?

B：_____。

A：一刻钟以后，在饭店门口上车，可以吗？
B：_____。

A：去旅行，你要准备什么？
B：_____。

A：你明天不来上班吗？
B：_____。

四、用下面的词说时间：

Use the following words to talk about time：

正　差　过　零　刻　半
现在是_____。

0:00　0:05　1:00　3:10
4:15　5:30　7:45　8:45
12:55　12:00　13:03　16:30
20:08　21:15　23:50

五、用"不"或"没有"填空，然后作出回答：

Fill in the blanks with 不 or 没有，and then answer the questions：

1. 张师傅今天_____来上班吗？

2. 秘书昨天_____预订房间吗？

六、会话练习：

Situational conversation：

情景：给饭店总服务台或出租车公司打电话要一辆车。
Call the general reception of a hotel or a taxi company for a taxi.

七、阅读下面的一段话，然后用拼音把这段话写出来：

Read the following passage and then put it into phonetic notation：

经理要秘书小王安排一辆车。一刻钟以后，小王打电话给经理，说车已经安排好了，请经理一刻钟以后在饭店大门口上车。经理问："是张师傅开车吗？"小王说："张师傅没有来上班，是饭店的车。"经理很高兴，说："知道了。"

第十课　今天是她的生日
Lesson 10　It Is Her Birthday Today

课文
Text

A:啊,好漂亮的鲜花!
B:给你!
A:送给我?小姐,你……
B:这是我替你买的。
A:我没叫你买花啊?
B:喂,噢,是钱太太。他在,您等等。经理,你的电话。

A:喂,亲爱的,有事吗?
B:现在几点了?
A:现在整六点。
B:你还不回家?
A:啊,对不起,晚上我还有一个约会。
B:你忘了今天是什么日子?
A:10月30日,星期五。

B：谁问你这个了！

A：小王，我太太刚才打电话，好像很生气。
B：为什么？
A：她问我，今天是什么日子。
B：你怎么说？
A：我说，今天是10月30日，星期五。
B：你太太就挂电话了？
A：是。我说错日子了？
B：没错。
A：她为什么生气呢？
B：今天是你太太的生日，我的大经理！
A：哦，天啦！谢谢你替我买的鲜花！请给我取消约会。

汉语拼音课文
Text in *Pinyin*

A：À, hǎo piàoliang de xiānhuā!
B：Gěi nǐ!
A：Sòng gěi wǒ? Xiǎojie, nǐ...
B：Zhè shì wǒ tì nǐ mǎi de.
A：Wǒ méi jiào nǐ mǎi huā a?
B：Wèi, ō, shì Qián tàitai. Tā zài, nín děngdeng. Jīnglǐ, nǐ de diànhuà.

A：Wèi, qīn'ài de, yǒu shì ma?

B: Xiànzài jǐ diǎn le?

A: Xiànzài zhěng liù diǎn.

B: Nǐ hái bù huí jiā?

A: À, duìbuqǐ, wǎnshang wǒ hái yǒu yī gè yuēhuì.

B: Nǐ wàng le jīntiān shì shénme rìzi?

A: Shí yuè sānshí rì, xīngqīwǔ.

B: Shuí wèn nǐ zhè gè le!

A: Xiǎo Wáng, wǒ tàitai gāngcái dǎ diànhuà, hǎoxiàng hěn shēngqì.

B: Wèishénme?

A: Tā wèn wǒ, jīntiān shì shénme rìzi.

B: Nǐ zěnme shuō?

A: Wǒ shuō, jīntiān shì shí yuè sānshí rì, xīngqīwǔ.

B: Nǐ tàitai jiù guà diànhuà le?

A: Shì. Wǒ shuō cuò rìzi le?

B: Méi cuò.

A: Tā wèishénme shēngqì ne?

B: Jīntiān shì nǐ tàitai de shēngrì, wǒ de dà jīnglǐ!

A: Ò, tiān la! Xièxie nǐ tì wǒ mǎi de xiānhuā! Qǐng gěi wǒ qǔxiāo yuēhuì.

生词
New Words

1. 鲜花　　xiānhuā　　fresh flowers

2.	漂亮	piàoliang	beautiful, pretty, good-looking
3.	送	sòng	deliver, give
4.	替	tì	take the place of; for
5.	买	mǎi	buy, purchase
6.	亲爱的	qīn'ài de	dear
7.	还	hái	even, also; in addition (expressing discovery or emphasis)
8.	回	huí	return, go back, reply
9.	家	jiā	home
10.	约会	yuēhuì	appointment
11.	忘	wàng	forget
12.	日子	rìzi	date, day
13.	月	yuè	month, moon
14.	日	rì	day, sun
15.	星期	xīngqī	week
16.	好像	hǎoxiàng	seem, be like
17.	生气	shēngqì	get angry, take offence
18.	为什么	wèishénme	why
19.	挂	guà	hang, put up, hang up
20.	大	dà	big, large, great
21.	生日	shēngrì	birthday
22.	天	tiān	sky, day
23.	啦	la	(auxiliary used to indicate exclamation or interrogation)
24.	取消	qǔxiāo	cancel, abolish

注释
Notes

一、"好",副词,放在动词或形容词前,强调程度,意思和"多么"差不多,表达一种感叹语气。例如:

好, as an adverb, is placed before a verb or an adjective to emphasize the degree. Its meaning is similar to 多么, expressing an exclamatory mood.

1. 这花好漂亮!
2. 她好高兴啊!
3. 秘书小姐好客气啊!
4. 他太太好生气啊!

二、"还",副词,表示行为、动作或某种情况维持不变。例如:

还, as an adverb, indicates that an action, movement or situation remains unchanged.

1. 他们还没下班。
2. 他还生我的气呢!
3. 他还没有女朋友。
4. 我还没有给她打电话。

"还",表示在某种程度或范围以外,有所增加或补充。例如:
还 also expresses addition or supplement beyond a certain degree or scope.

1. 他有一个中国朋友,还有一个美国朋友。
2. 昨天,我见到了钱经理,还见到了他的太太。

3. 钱经理买了鲜花,还买了生日蛋糕。

三、"就",副词,说明时间。当两件事先后连续发生,在说明后一件事的句子中用"就"字,表示后一件事紧接着前一件事发生。例如:

就 is an adverb indicating time. When two things happen one after the other, 就 is used before the second event, meaning that it happens right after the first event.

1. 刚到五点钟,他就回家了。
2. 老板进门就叫秘书去买花。
3. 他见了老师就问问题。
4. 我有了钱就去旅行。

补充生词
Additional New Words

星期一	xīngqīyī	Monday
星期二	xīngqī'èr	Tuesday
星期三	xīngqīsān	Wednesday
星期四	xīngqīsì	Thursday
星期五	xīngqīwǔ	Friday
星期六	xīngqīliù	Saturday
星期日(星期天)	xīngqīrì(xīngqītiān)	Sunday
周末	zhōumò	weekend
上星期	shàng xīngqī	last week
下星期	xià xīngqī	next week
年	nián	year
蛋糕	dàngāo	cake

练习
Exercises

一、**替换练习:**
Substitution drills:

A:<u>你</u>的生日是什么时候?
B:<u>5月15日</u>是<u>我</u>的生日。

你弟弟	8月25日	我弟弟
你爸爸	1月1日	我爸爸
你妈妈	7月30日	我妈妈
你女朋友	5月16日	我女朋友

A:<u>星期五</u>晚上,你有约会吗?
B:没有。<u>星期六</u>晚上我有一个约会。

今天	明天
星期一	星期三
星期二	星期五
星期六	星期日

A:你去哪儿?
B:我回<u>家</u>。

| 学校 |
| 宿舍 |
| 教室 |
| 办公室 |

A:你送她什么?
B:我送她<u>鲜花</u>。

| 生日蛋糕 |
| 一本书 |
| 一些钱 |
| 一辆车 |

二、**把下面的词组成句子:**
Unscramble the following into normal sentences:

1. 这 你 吗 约会 是

2. 她 约会 了 取消

3. 今天 生日 是 的 我

4. 请 电话 挂 你 别

5. 你 我 替 老师 问问 去

三、朗读下面的会话,然后替换划线部分的词语再朗读:
Read the following dialogues aloud, and then change the underlined parts and read them again:

A:啊,<u>经理</u>,今天你好漂亮!
B:谢谢。
A:你知道为什么吗?
B:我知道,<u>今天是我的生日</u>。

A:经理,刚才你<u>太太</u>来电话了。
B:有什么事吗?
A:她谢谢你送给她<u>鲜花</u>。
B:我没送给她<u>鲜花</u>啊?
A:是我替你买的。
B:为什么?
A:你忘了,今天是你<u>太太</u>生日!
B:哦,谢谢你!

101

四、完成对话：

Complete the following dialogues：

A：你知道你父母的生日吗？
B：_____。

A：你父母的生日你送鲜花吗？
B：_____。

A：你为什么给你的朋友打电话？
B：_____。

A：她为什么生你的气？
B：_____。

A：你找经理什么事,预约了吗？
B：_____。

五、指出下列句子中"还"的不同用法：

Point out how 还 is used in the following sentences：

1. 什么时候了,你还没有预订房间？

2. 给我钱,还给我一辆车。

3. 他找错了钱,还忘了说对不起。

4. 经理周末还工作。

5. 你还有什么事吗？

六、用下列词语和副词"就"各造一个句子：

Make sentences with the following expressions and the adverb 就：

1. 买了鲜花　　回家

2. 有钱　　　　买车

3. 到了　　　　打电话

4. 做错事　　　生气

5. 上班　　　　忘了

七、会话练习：

Situational conversations：

情景1：打电话，为朋友预订生日蛋糕。
Make a phone call to order a birthday cake for a friend.

情景2：给朋友送生日蛋糕和鲜花。
Send the birthday cake and flowers to your friend.

八、给下面的拼音标上调号，然后朗读几遍：

Mark the tones of the following passage and then read it aloud for several times：

Jintian, shi Qian taitai de shengri. Qian taitai gei Qian jingli da dianhua, wen ta shenme shihou hui jia. Qian jingli shuo, ta wanshang hai you yuehui, yao hen wan cai hui jia. Qian taitai hen shengqi, yi xia jiu guale dianhua. Qian jingli wen mishu xiao Wang, ta zuo cuo shenme shi le, xiao Wang shuo: "Wo de da jingli, jintian shi ni taitai de shengri!" Qian jingli shuo: "Ou, wo de shangdi! Wo zenme wang le!"

第十一课　你想做什么(一)
Lesson 11　What Do You Want to Do (1)

课文
Text

在课内

王老师:同学们,你们大家都认识了吧?
杰　克:我先做一下自我介绍。
山　口:不用介绍,我知道你叫杰克,美国人。
杰　克:我也知道你叫山口,日本人。
珍　妮:我们互相都认识。
山　口:我还知道,珍妮来中国学习汉语。
珍　妮:可是,你知道我为什么学习汉语吗?
山　口:那还用问,以后好在中国做生意!
珍　妮:对!也不对!
杰　克:这是什么意思?
珍　妮:杰克,我问你,你为什么学习汉语?
杰　克:我喜欢交朋友。

珍　妮：山口，你呢？
山　口：我？我爱玩。不学汉语，怎么在中国旅行？

王老师：同学们，你们刚才说都认识珍妮，对吧？
杰　克：是。我们都认识珍妮。
王老师：你们了解珍妮吗？
山　口：还不太了解。
珍　妮：我们互相都还不太了解。
山　口：珍妮刚才说的话，我和杰克就不太明白。
王老师：珍妮，你学习汉语不是为了做生意吗？
珍　妮：当服务员也是在做生意。
杰　克：你不想当服务员？
珍　妮：不！
山　口：当秘书？
珍　妮：不！
杰　克：那你想做什么？

生词
New Words

1. 想　　xiǎng　　think, want to, would like to
2. 大家　dàjiā　　all, everybody
3. 都　　dōu　　　all; even
4. 先　　xiān　　 earlier, at first
5. 自己　zìjǐ　　 oneself
6. 用　　yòng　　 use, need

7.	互相	hùxiāng	mutually, each other
8.	学习	xuéxí	study, learn
9.	汉语	Hànyǔ	Chinese
10.	可是	kěshì	but, yet, however
11.	意思	yìsi	meaning, idea, interest
12.	喜欢	xǐhuan	like, love
13.	交	jiāo	associate with
14.	爱	ài	love
15.	玩	wán	play, have fun
16.	了解	liǎojiě	understand, acquaint oneself with
17.	太	tài	too, very
18.	话	huà	word, talk
19.	和	hé	and
20.	明白	míngbai	clear, obvious
21.	为了	wèile	for; in order to, for the sake of
22.	当	dāng	work as, serve as, be
23.	服务员	fúwùyuán	attendant
24.	那(么)	nà(me)	then, in that case

注释
Notes

一、"用",动词,意思是使用、利用工具、手段做事或实现某种目的。例如:

用, as a verb, indicates the use or utilization of a tool or a means to do something or to achieve a certain aim.

  1. 这是用钱买的鲜花。
  2. 他用旅行支票换现金。
  3. 他用公司的车送儿子上学。

"用",意思是需要,多用否定形式"不用",就是不需要的意思。例如:

用 also means "need", and is often used in the negative form. 不用 means "no need".

  1. 今天是星期天,不用上班。
  2. 不用问,她就是你的女朋友!
  3. 不用打电话,我自己去找他。

二、"在",介词,跟表处所的名词或词组组成介词短语,在句子中作定语、状语或补语。例如:

在, as a preposition, forms a prepositional phrase with a noun or an expression of place, which functions as an attribute, an adverbial, or a complement.

  1. 小王在一家公司上班。
  2. 在北京的留学生都交了中国朋友。
  3. 出租车停在饭店的门口。

"在"或"正在",还是时间副词,表示行为、动作处在进行的状态。"在"和"正在"的意义、用法差不多,"正在"更加强调动作进行的时间。所以,"在"的前面往往还有时间词而不觉得重复,"正在"前面则常常不需要时间词。例如:

在 or 正在 are time adverbs, indicating that the motion or action is in progress. The meaning and usage of 在 and 正在 are similar, but 正在 lays more emphasis on the time of the action in progress. Therefore, an expression of time can be used before 在 without being repetitive, but there is no need to have any expression of time before 正在.

1. 我们现在在上课,不要说话。
2. 上个月,他在学习汉语,没有做生意。
3. 我正在打电话的时候,他进来了。
4. 我正在上班,你自己去买花吧!

补充生词
Additional New Words

英语	Yīngyǔ	English
法语	Fǎyǔ	French
日语	Rìyǔ	Japanese
以前	yǐqián	before, previously

练习
Exercises

一、替换练习:
Substitution drills:

A：你想做什么？
B：我想做生意。

玩
去旅行
当老师
当银行经理

A：你喜欢什么？
B：我喜欢旅行。

开车玩
学习汉语
朋友送我鲜花
交中国朋友

A：你在做什么？
B：我正在学习。

工作
打电话
学习开车
想她说的话

二、把下面的词组成句子：

Unscramble the following into normal sentences：

1. 你　汉语　为什么　学习

2. 我们　大家　她　都　喜欢

3. 这　自己　我　是　事　的

4. 我　她　了解　不　还

5. 我　明白　你　话　不　说　的

三、朗读下面的会话,然后替换划线部分的词语,再朗读:

Read the following dialogues aloud, and then change the underlined parts and read them again:

A:同学们,你们互相都<u>认识</u>了吧?
B:<u>是</u>,我们不用自我介绍了。
A:你们为什么来<u>中国</u>?
B:为了<u>学习汉语</u>。
A:你喜欢<u>学习汉语</u>吗?
B:还可以。
A:你这是什么意思?
B:就是这个意思。
A:我不太明白。
B:还可以就是还可以。

四、完成对话:

Complete the following dialogues:

A:你为什么学习汉语?
B:＿＿＿＿＿＿＿＿＿＿。

A:你了解你的中国朋友吗?
B:＿＿＿＿＿＿＿＿＿＿。

A:你喜欢交什么朋友?
B:＿＿＿＿＿＿＿＿＿＿。

A:请问,你喜欢做什么?
B:＿＿＿＿＿＿＿＿＿＿。

五、把下面的词语扩展成句子：

Expand the following into sentences：

1. 互相学习

2. 互相了解

3. 互相打电话

4. 互相约会

5. 互相问问题

六、用下面提供的词语，完成句子：

Complete the following sentences：

1. 以前他在_____
   现在他在_____

2. 他先用汉语_____
   后用英语_____

3. 以前经理上班请司机_____
   现在不用司机_____

4. 不用客气，你不明白的话，可以_____

5. 他刚学习汉语，_____

七、请介绍你喜欢什么，不喜欢什么。

Talk about your likes and dislikes.

八、会话练习：

Situational conversation：

情景：A 与 B 互相问对方想做什么。

A and B ask each other about what they want to do.

九、阅读下面的一段话，然后用拼音把这段话写出来：

Read the following passage and then put it into phonetic notation：

同学们正在上课，老师想知道他们是不是都互相认识了。同学们说，都认识了，可是还不太了解。比如（bǐrú for example），大家学好汉语以后都想做什么呢？杰克说，他学好汉语是为了交朋友；山口说，她学好汉语是为了在中国旅行；珍妮想做什么呢？珍妮说了，可大家还是不明白。

第十二课　你想做什么(二)
Lesson 12　What Do You Want to Do (2)

课文
Text

在课外

服务员:欢迎！欢迎！请进！
刘经理:王老师,你好！
王老师:你是……
刘经理:王老师不认识我了?我是您的学生刘亮啊！
王老师:是你啊,刘亮！你也是来玩的吗?
刘经理:不。我是这个酒吧的经理。
王老师:哦? 我记得,你刚工作三年,就当经理了?
刘经理:老师忘了,我是学经济管理的?
王老师:啊,对,你还很努力,学得很不错！

刘经理:王老师,你们喝点儿什么?别客气!
王老师:随便,茶、可口可乐、橘汁,都可以。
杰　克:我要啤酒。
刘经理:好的。服务员!
珍　妮:刘先生,你刚工作三年就当经理了,是真的?
刘经理:是真的。
杰　克:珍妮,你也想当酒吧经理?
珍　妮:怎么,不行啊?我还想当老板、总裁呢!
杰　克:行,当然行!不过……
珍　妮:不过什么?
杰　克:你得(děi)先到这儿来当服务员!
珍　妮:为什么?
杰　克:先学走,再学跑啊!
山　口:珍妮不学走也会跑!哈……

生词
New Words

1.	欢迎	huānyíng	welcome
2.	酒吧	jiǔbā	bar, barroom
3.	记得	jìde	remember
4.	工作	gōngzuò	work, job
5.	经济	jīngjì	economy
6.	管理	guǎnlǐ	manage; management
7.	努力	nǔlì	make great efforts, exert oneself

8.	得	de	(auxiliary used to link up a complement indicating result or degree)
9.	喝	hē	drink
10.	随便	suíbiàn	casual, random; any
11.	茶	chá	tea
12.	可口可乐	Kěkǒu Kělè	Coca Cola
13.	橘汁	júzhī	orange juice
14.	啤酒	píjiǔ	beer
15.	真	zhēn	true, real, indeed
16.	老板	lǎobǎn	boss
17.	总裁	zǒngcái	president
18.	当然	dāngrán	of course
19.	不过	búguò	but
20.	得	děi	(auxiliary expressing a volitional or factual necessity)
21.	走	zǒu	walk
22.	会	huì	can, be able to, be good at
23.	跑	pǎo	run

专名

Proper Noun

| 刘亮 | Liú Liàng | Liu Liang |

注释
Notes

一、"得"(de),结构助词,用在动词或形容词的后边,连接表示结果或程度的补语。例如:

得 is a structural auxiliary word used after a verb or an adjective to link up a complement indicating result or degree.

1. 你的汉语说得真好。
2. 他的生意做得很不错。
3. 他们玩得很高兴。
4. 这个酒吧管理得太好了。
5. 安娜高兴得说个不停。

二、"得"(děi),助动词,口语里常用,表示意志上或事实上的必要。例如:

得 is an auxiliary verb which is often used in spoken Chinese to express a volitional or factual necessity.

1. 我得好好谢谢你。
2. 你得多练习。
3. 现在八点钟了,我得去上班了。
4. 开车的时候,得系好安全带。

注意:"得"的否定形式是"不用"、"不要"、"不必"。不说"不得"。例如:

The negative form of 得 is 不用, 不要, or 不必, but we don't use 不得.

1. 她得工作。

2. 她不用工作。
3. 我得走了!
4. 你现在不要走!
5. 你现在还不必走!

补充生词
Additional New Words

咖啡	kāfēi	coffee
矿泉水	kuàngquánshuǐ	mineral water
饮料	yǐnliào	beverage, drink
酒	jiǔ	alcoholic drink, wine, liquor
葡萄酒	pútaojiǔ	grape wine
杯	bēi	cup
瓶	píng	bottle
听	tīng	tin, can

练习
Exercises

一、替换练习:

Substitution drills:

A:喝点儿什么?
B:有<u>茶</u>吗? 我喜欢喝<u>茶</u>。
A:有,你等等。
B:谢谢!

咖啡
啤酒
矿泉水
可口可乐

A:你想喝点儿什么?
B:随便。
A:那就喝杯咖啡吧?
B:好的。

| 茶 |
| (点儿)饮料 |
| (点儿)酒 |
| (点儿)可乐 |

A:我想做生意。
B:那你得有钱。

去旅行	有时间
买汽车	先学开车
当总裁	学经济管理
进公司工作	了解公司

二、把下面的词组成句子:

Unscramble the following into normal sentences:

1. 你 我 来 工作 酒吧 欢迎 的

2. 我 喝 饮料 想 点儿

3. 刚 三个月 汉语 我 学

4. 他 努力 很 工作

5. 你们 在 随便 公司 看看 可以

三、完成对话:

Complete the following dialogues:

A:_____?
B:我想喝杯咖啡。

A:你认识这个酒吧的老板吗？
B:_____,他是_____。

A:请问你是学什么的？
B:_____？

A:你以后想做什么？
B:_____？

四、模仿例句说话：

Complete the following sentences according to the example：
例句：要学开车,得请师傅。

1. 想当老板,得

2. 做生意,得

3. 要会跑,先得

4. 今天是太太生日,经理得

五、用结构助词"得"完成句子：

Complete the following sentences：

1. 经理送秘书鲜花,秘书高兴得_____。

2. 小谢刚学了三个月汉语,已经说得_____。

3. 这个公司你管理得_____。

4. 张师傅开车开得_____。

5. 今天是老师的生日，大家玩得_____。

六、会话练习：

Situational conversations：

情景 1：请一个朋友去饭店或酒吧喝点什么。
Invite a friend to a restaurant or a bar to have a drink.

情景 2：几个朋友或同事在一起，谈谈自己的工作，以前学什么，以后想做什么。
Several friends or colleagues gather together to talk about their work, what they learned before, and what they want to do in future.

七、给下面的拼音标上调号，然后朗读几遍：

Mark the tones of the following passage and then read it aloud for several times：

Yitian, Wang laoshi he tongxue men qu yi ge jiuba. Jiuba de laoban shi ta de xuesheng Liu Liang. Liu Liang shi xue jingji de, gang gongzuo san nian jiu dang laoban le. Zhenni wen："Zhe shi zhen de?" Liu Liang shuo："Zhe shi zhen de." Zhenni ting le hen gaoxing, shuo："Wo ye xiang dang laoban, hai xiang dang zongcai ne!"

第十三课　你会说中国话吗（一）

Lesson 13 Do You Speak Chinese（1）

课文
Text

在课内

王老师：同学们，你们谁会说中国话？
杰　克：我会说，但是说得不好。
珍　妮：我才开始学习汉语，只会说一点儿。
王老师：我的问题不是这个意思，我知道你们都会说一点儿汉语了。
珍　妮：那么老师的意思是什么呢？
王老师：我先考考你们，怎么请求别人帮助。
珍　妮：好的，我来试试。

珍　妮：喂，老头，北京大学在哪儿？
杰　克：喂，谁姓"喂"？你会不会叫人？
珍　妮：啊，对不起！老大爷，请问北京大学在哪儿?
王老师:这就对了,老大爷一定会高高兴兴告诉你。
杰　克:是,请求别人帮助,应该有礼貌。
王老师:好,再来一次。

山　口:开车的,去长城饭店!
杰　克:不去!
山　口:喂,你怎么走了?
杰　克:他当然要走啦,谁让你叫他"开车的"!
山　口:我该怎么叫?
杰　克:叫"师傅"呀!"师傅,去长城饭店!"
山　口:对,这样有礼貌,司机还会不高兴吗?
王老师:好,你们明白我的问题是什么意思了吗?
珍　妮:明白了。

生词
New Words

1. 但是　　dànshì　　but, yet, nevertheless
2. 考(试)　kǎo(shì)　exam, test
3. 才　　　cái　　　only; not until
4. 开始　　kāishǐ　　begin, start
5. 只　　　zhǐ　　　only, merely
6. 一点儿　yīdiǎnr　　a bit, a little
7. 试　　　shì　　　try, test
8. 请求　　qǐngqiú　　ask, request

9.	别人	biérén	other people, others
10.	帮助	bāngzhù	help; assistance
11.	老头	lǎotóu	old man, old chap
12.	老	lǎo	old
13.	大爷	dàye	uncle, father's elder brother
14.	一定	yīdìng	certainly, surely; fixed; certain
15.	告诉	gàosu	tell, let know
16.	应该	yīnggāi	should, ought to
17.	礼貌	lǐmào	courtesy, politeness, manners
18.	再	zài	again, once more
19.	让	ràng	let, make
20.	次	cì	time, occurence
21.	这样	zhèyàng	such, this way, like this

专名
Proper Nouns

北京大学	Běijīng Dàxué	Beijing University
长城饭店	Chángchéng Fàndiàn	the Great Wall Hotel

注释
Notes

一、"点",量词,在表示少量时,必须儿化,数词限于"一"、"半"。口语中"一"常常省略。例如:

点 is a measure word. When it is used to mean a little, it

has the suffixation of a nonsyllabic r, causing a retroflexion of the preceding vowel, and the numerals used with it are restricted to "one", and "half". In spoken Chinese, the numeral "one" is often omitted.

1. 学了一点儿汉语。
2. 买了一点儿蛋糕。
3. 换了一点儿钱。
4. 我一点儿也不喜欢喝酒。
5. 她一点儿也不会做生意。

二、许多动词可以重叠使用,重叠后的动词,有尝试、经历时间短暂等附加意义。单音节动词的重叠形式是AA,或A一A;双音节动词的重叠形式是ABAB。例如:

Many verbs can be used in a duplicate form, which suggests a try or a short duration of the action. Monosyllabic verbs, when duplicated, follow the pattern of AA or with 一 (one) inserted in between. The duplication of disyllabic verbs follows the pattern of ABAB.

坐坐(坐一坐)　　　介绍介绍
等等(等一等)　　　学习学习
问问(问一问)　　　准备准备
说说(说一说)　　　欢迎欢迎

有些形容词也可以重叠,表示程度加深。重叠的形式是AABB。例如:
Some adjectives can also be duplicated to indicate the deepening of the degree, and the pattern is AABB.

高高兴兴　　　客客气气
明明白白　　　漂漂亮亮
安安全全

三、"老",可以用作词头,也可以用作词尾,用来称呼老人,常表达出一种亲热、尊敬的口气。例如:

老 can be used as a prefix or a suffix to address an old person, which often carries with it a tone of closeness or respect.

老大爷　　老大娘　　老师傅　　老同志
王老　　　钱老　　　谢老　　　您老

但下面的称呼,用于年龄相近的同辈、同事:

But the following addresses are used among peers or colleagues:

老王　　　老钱　　　老谢

补充生词
Additional New Words

劳驾	láojià	excuse me; may I trouble you; would you please
大娘	dàniáng	aunt; wife of father's elder brother
同志	tóngzhì	comrade
路	lù	road, path, way
声	shēng	sound, voice, tone
句	jù	sentence

练习
Exercises

一、替换练习:

Substitution drills:

A:你会<u>开车</u>吗?
B:我不会,<u>我的秘书</u>会。

说英语	杰克
做生意	刘亮
喝茶	我的中国朋友
开葡萄酒瓶	酒吧服务员

A:我可以帮你做点儿什么吗?
B:请问<u>在哪儿换钱</u>?

| 怎么打电话 |
| 怎么去国际邮局 |
| 你们经理在哪儿 |
| 在哪儿可以买到鲜花 |

二、把下面的词组成句子:

Unscramble the following into normal sentences:

1. 我 汉语 说 会 一点儿

2. 我 明白 的 意思 你

3. 你 问题 应该 有 告诉 我 什么

4. 明天 有 考试 我们

5. 我们 帮助 应该 大家 互相

三、完成对话：

Complete the following dialogues：

A：你会说汉语吗？
B：_____。

A：叫司机"开车的"，司机会高兴吗？
B：_____，应该叫_____。

A：怎么问路才对？
B：_____。

A：看见老人应该怎么称呼？
B：_____。

A：你是什么时候开始学习汉语的？
B：_____。

四、用"一点儿"完成下面的句子：

Complete the following sentences with 一点儿：

1. 路上　　　　　　堵车
2. 现在十点　　　　过
3. 今天经理　　　　生气
4. 服务员说话　　　不礼貌
5. 先生，请你说话　客气

五、用动词或形容词重叠形式完成下列句子：

Complete the following sentences with the duplicate form of verbs or adjectives:

1. 我有问题,请你_____。(帮)
2. 后天我去旅行,要_____。(准备)
3. 这句汉语你说得不对,得_____。(问)
4. 这句汉语你一定会说,请_____。(试)
5. 老师要_____,谁知道这句汉语怎么说才对。(考)
6. 山口的汉语说得真不错,大家_____。(明白)
7. 秘书小姐对什么人都_____。(客气)
8. 今天是她的生日,我们得_____。(高兴)
9. 这个约会不应该_____就取消。(随便)
10. 有礼貌的、_____的秘书小姐大家都喜欢。(漂亮)

六、用你学会的汉语谈谈怎么说,怎么做是没有礼貌;怎么说,怎么做是有礼貌的?

Talk about what is polite and what is impolite in speaking and in acting.

七、会话练习:

Situational conversations:

情景1:打电话给服务台预订房间(有礼貌和没有礼貌各表演一次)

Call the reception to book a room (once polite, and once impolite).

情景2:问路(有礼貌和没有礼貌各表演一次)

Ask the way (once polite, and once impolite).

八、阅读下面的一段话，然后用拼音把这段话写出来：

Read the following passage and then put it into phonetic notation：

说话，要会说。说的话不好听，别人听了会不高兴的。比如，问路，叫出租车，请求别人帮助，都要有礼貌。叫人的时候，应该叫一声"大爷"、"大娘"、"师傅"、"同志"或者"先生"、"小姐"；说一句"请问"、"劳驾"。见人就叫"喂"、"喂"的，这样没有礼貌，谁还会高高兴兴帮助你？

第十四课　你会说中国话吗（二）

Lesson 14　Do You Speak Chinese（2）

课文
Text

在课外

珍妮:杰克,昨天的汉语课真有意思!

杰克:是。想说好汉语,真不容易!

珍妮:我们一起练习练习吧!

杰克:好的。我当商店售货员,你当顾客,怎么样?

珍妮:好,开始!

杰克:小姐,欢迎您来购物!

珍妮:欢迎购物？不买,随便看看,就不行吗？

杰克:啊,欢迎! 您请随便!

珍妮:看,你说话不得体,顾客生气了。

杰克:好,我们再试试。

杰克：小姐,您要点儿什么?
珍妮：什么话? 我是来要东西的吗?
杰克：我不是那个意思,请不要误会。
珍妮：是我误会了你,还是你不会说话?
杰克：啊,对不起!

杰克：你看,我又说错了。
珍妮：你不能说"要什么"。
杰克：我应该怎么说?
珍妮：应该说,小姐,您想买点儿什么。
杰克：不对! 不对!"我不买,看看就不行?"
珍妮：嗯,要是这么说,顾客也会生气的。
杰克：那该怎么说呢?
珍妮：啊,太难了,我也不会了!

生词
New Words

1. 容易　　róngyì　　　　easy, liable
2. 一起　　yīqǐ　　　　　together, altogether, in the same place
3. 练习　　liànxí　　　　practice
4. 售货员　shòuhuòyuán　shop assistant, salesclerk
5. 顾客　　gùkè　　　　　customer
6. 购物　　kòuwù　　　　purchase, buy, go shopping
7. 得体　　détǐ　　　　　appropriate; befitting one's

			position or suited to the occasion
8.	要	yào	want, ask for, wish, must
9.	东西	dōngxi	think
10.	误会	wùhuì	misunderstand, mistake
11.	又	yòu	again; also
12.	能	néng	may, can, be able to; ability
13.	要是	yàoshì	if, in case; suppose
14.	难	nán	difficult, hard, troublesome
15.	嗯	ng	(interjection used to show different tones)

注释
Notes

一、"又"和"再",两个都是副词,都可以表示同一个动作、行为的重复,但用法不同。对于已实现的行为或动作,只能用"又";而对未实现、或将要实现、或假想的动作、行为,则要用"再"。请认真比较下面的句子:

又 and 再 are both adverbs to express repetition of the same motion or action, but they are used differently. For a motion or action that has been fulfilled, only 又 can be used. For a motion or action that has not been fulfilled, or one that will be fulfilled in the future, or a fictitious one, 再 should be used.

1. 他前天来了,昨天又来了。
2. 请你明天再来。

3. 时候还早,再坐会儿吧!
4. 他真的又坐下了。

5. 你已经喝了很多啤酒,可不能再喝了。
6. 他喝了很多啤酒,又吃了很多蛋糕。

7. 我去了北京饭店,再去长城饭店,要花不少车费。
8. 他早上没吃东西,拿上书,又带上笔,就去教室了。

上面的前六个例子中的"又"和"再",都不能互换。后面两个例子中的"又"和"再",可以互换,但原句表达的行为有先有后,换了以后,意思就不同了。

In the first six of the examples above, 又 and 再 cannot replace each other. In the last two examples, 再 can be replaced by 又, but the original sentences imply a sequence of the actions, and there is a change of meaning after the replacement.

二、"要",动词,意思是需要、希望得到。例如:
要, as a verb, expresses that one needs or hopes to get something.

1. 人不能没有钱,谁不要钱!
2. 他要了一杯可口可乐。
3. 一年要多少学费?

"要",助动词,放在谓语前面,表示愿望或事实上的需要。例如:
要 is also an auxiliary verb to be placed before the predicate to express a wish or a factual necessity.

1. 你要好好学汉语。

2. 我要去买蛋糕。
3. 请不要大声说话!

"要"、"要是",连词,表示假设。"要是"多用于口语。例如:
要 or 要是 is a conjunction expressing a supposition. 要是 is used more often in spoken Chinese.

1. 他要不喜欢,你就别给他买。
2. 你要是能来,那就太好了。
3. 你要是不高兴听,我就不说了。

补充生词
Additional New Words

为	wèi	for, because of, for the sake of
效劳	xiàoláo	work for, work in the service of

练习
Exercises

一、**替换练习**:

Substitution drills:

A:我们一起去<u>商店</u>好吗?
B:对不起,我要去<u>邮局</u>。

教室	宿舍
喝咖啡	上班
学习汉语	找工作
问老师	打电话

A：你能帮我<u>叫</u>辆出租车吗？
B：对不起，我不能，你自己<u>叫</u>吧！

| 练习一下口语 |
| 预订一个房间 |
| 找一下饭店经理 |
| 送一支鲜花给安娜 |

二、把下面的词组成句子：

Unscramble the following into normal sentences：

1. 你　真　说话　有意思　的

2. 汉语　难　吗　很　学习

3. 星期天　我们　商店　购物　去

4. 我　买　东西　去　商店　点儿

5. 我　你　意思　误会　了　对不起　的

三、完成对话：

Complete the following dialogues：

A：你什么时候去商店买东西？
B：_____。

A：商店的售货员都很有礼貌吗？
B：_____。

A：_____？
B：我随便看看。

A：我能学好汉语吗？
B：当然，_____。

四、选择"又"或"再"填入下列各句：

Fill in the blanks with 又 or 再：

1. 他_____开始学习汉语了。
2. 老板想自己先去中国旅行，以后_____让太太去。
3. 我刚换了100美元，_____换50美元。
4. 秘书小姐为老板预订了房间，_____预订了车。
5. 司机已经开了5个小时车了，不能_____开车了。
6. 他喝了_____喝，已经不能_____喝了。
7. 他_____来中国的时候，老朋友都不在了。
8. 他已经听明白了，你就不要_____说了。

五、模仿例句说话：

Make sentences according to the example：

例：要是没有他的帮助，我就不能来中国。

1. 要是　　钱　　　　旅行
2. 要是　　效劳　　　高兴
3. 要　　　喜欢　　　买
4. 要　　　告诉　　　生气
5. 要想　　学好汉语　就要

六、用下列词汇说一段话（4—5句）：

Say 4 to 5 sentences, using the following words：

汉语　　难　　容易　　学习　　一点儿
一定　　能　　练习

七、会话练习：
Situational conversations：

情景：几个顾客在商店购物，一个顾客说话很得体，一个顾客很没礼貌，一个顾客会说一点儿汉语，听不明白，也说不明白。
售货员小姐怎么为他们效劳？
Several customers are shopping. One customer speaks in appropriate terms. One is rude. One can speak a little Chinese, but he doesn't understand what is said to him and cannot make himself understood.
How would the salesgirl serve them?

八、给下面的拼音标上调号，然后朗读几遍：
Mark the tones of the following passage and then read it aloud for several times：

Yitian, Zhenni he Jieke zai ke wai lianxi shuo Hanyu, Jieke dang shangdian fuwuyuan, Zhenni dang guke. Zhenni qu mai dongxi. Keshi, zhege fuwuyuan haoxiang bu tai hui shuohua, zenme shuo, guke dou shengqi, zheyang zenme neng zuo hao shengyi ne? Ou, Jieke he Zhenni, hai yinggai haohao lianxi shuo Hanyu.

第十五课　你会买东西吗(一)
Lesson 15　Do You Know How to Make Purchases (1)

课文
Text

在课内
王老师:同学们,你们会买东西吗？
珍　妮:会。一手交钱,一手交货。
杰　克:这么简单？
王老师:你们试试,看看是不是这么简单。

杰　克:喂,苹果多少钱一斤？
珍　妮:杰克,不能在这儿买。
杰　克:怎么？你不会砍价？
珍　妮:不是不会砍价,是不能在这儿砍价！
杰　克:为什么？
珍　妮:这个卖苹果的,是我朋友的爸爸！

珍　妮:喂,苹果多少钱一斤？

小　贩：十二块三斤。
珍　妮：十块三斤,卖不卖?
小　贩：十块两斤半!
珍　妮：什么?还是四块钱一斤?
杰　克：小老板,你真会蒙人!
珍　妮：十块钱三斤,不卖,我们走了!
小　贩：好,好,十块三斤!

珍　妮：怎么样?我砍掉他两块钱!
杰　克：你买了几斤苹果?
珍　妮：三斤呀!
杰　克：你去称称,最多两斤半!
珍　妮：真的?那还是四块钱一斤呀!
杰　克：怎么样,买东西不简单吧?

生词
New Words

1.	手	shǒu	hand
2.	货	huò	goods, commodity
3.	简单	jiǎndān	simple
4.	苹果	píngguǒ	apple
5.	斤	jīn	half a kilo
6.	砍	kǎn	cut, chop
7.	价(格)	jià(gé)	price
8.	小贩	xiǎofàn	peddler

9.	两	liǎng	two
10.	卖	mài	sell
11.	蒙人	mēngrén	cheating
12.	怎么样	zěnmeyàng	how; what's it like; in a certain way
13.	掉	diào	fall, drop, remove
14.	呀	ya	ah
15.	称	chēng	weigh
16.	最	zuì	most

注释
Notes

一、"会",助动词,表示有(没有)某种能力。例如:
会, an auxiliary verb, indicates having a certain ability.

1. 我会说汉语。
2. 她不会开车。
3. 王老师是个好老师,但不会做生意。

"会",也表示可能。例如:
会 also expresses possibility:

1. 你再等一会儿吧,他会来的。
2. 你不交钱,小贩不会交货给你。
3. 他是一个好人,蒙人的事,他不会做。

"能",也是助动词,表示有能力做某事,或条件、环境、情理允许做某事。例如:

能 is also an auxiliary verb, indicating the ability to do something, or that the conditions, circumstances, or accepted code of human conduct permit doing something.

1. 我能帮助你。
2. 这种苹果能卖5元钱一斤。
3. 他家里今天有事,不能来上班。
4. 经理不能没有秘书。

注意:"能"和"会"都是助动词,学生常常误用,要注意辨别这两个词的异同。"会"和"能",都可表示有能力做某事,这种情况下,两个词可以互换。例如:

Please note that both 能 and 会 are auxiliary verbs, and students often misuse them. Special attention should be paid to the similarities and differences between these two words. Both 会 and 能 can be used to express the ability to do something. Under such circumstances, these two words can be used interchangeably.

1. 小孩一岁半了,会说话了。
2. 小孩一岁半了,能说话了。

下面例子中的"能",表示条件、环境允许,或丧失的能力又恢复了,不能换用"会"。

能 in the following examples expresses permission by the conditions, or circumstances, or the recovery of a certain lost ability, and it cannot be replaced by 会.

1. 你会抽烟吗?
2. 我不会抽烟。
3. 我能(在办公室)抽烟吗?
4. 你不能抽烟。

5. 他来中国以后,会说汉语了。
6. 他来中国以后,(又)能说汉语了。(回美国以后不说汉语,忘了,现在回到中国,他又能说了。)

表示达到某种程度、水平、效率等,只能用"能",不能用"会"。例如:

To express reaching a certain extent, level or efficiency, only 能 can be used, and it cannot be replaced by 会.

1. 他能认800个汉语生词了。
2. 他的英语很好,能当大学英语老师。
3. 他三分钟能喝六瓶啤酒。

二、"两"和"二",都是数词"2",但"二"可以单独使用,"两"则不能。例如数数,要说"一、二、三",不能说"一、两、三"。但"二"在量词前边,一般要读成"两"。例如:

二 and 两 both indicate the numeral 2, but 二 can be used independently while 两 can't. For instance, when counting, we should say 一, 二, 三 and not 一, 两, 三. But when 二 is used before a measure word, it is generally pronounced as 两.

二个学生——读成 "liǎng ge xuésheng"
二个小时——读成 "liǎng ge xiǎoshí"

二元钱——读成 "liǎng yuán qián"

三、"怎么"和"怎么样",都是疑问代词,用来询问性质、状况、方式等,"怎么"常用作状语。"怎么样"常用作谓语,也可作状语。"怎么"作状语时,还可用来询问原因,但"怎么样"则没有这种用法。"怎么样",用来征求他人的意见和对他人或事物的评价,"怎么"则不能。

Both 怎么 and 怎么样 are interrogative pronouns. They are used to ask about the nature, condition, or way. 怎么 is often used as an adverbial. 怎么样 is often used as a predicate, or sometimes as an adverbial. When 怎么 is used as an adverbial, it can also be asking about the reason, but 怎么样 cannot be used this way. 怎么样 can be used to ask for others' opinions or comments on other people or things, while 怎么 cannot be used this way.

1. 他怎么还不来?
2. 我们怎么去长城?
3. 你的汉语学得怎么样了?
4. 这个服务员怎么样?好不好?

补充生词
Additional New Words

葡萄	pútao	grape
香蕉	xiāngjiāo	banana
西瓜	xīguā	watermelon
橘子	júzi	tangerine

岁	suì	year
抽烟	chōuyān	smoke

练习
Exercises

一、替换练习：

Substitution drills：

A：你会开车吗？
B：我会开车，但是我现在不能开车。
    我没有车了。

买车	没有钱
做生意	没有秘书
工作	还要学习
抽烟	正在售货

A：老板，买水果。
B：买什么水果？
A：苹果。
B：您买几斤？
A：二斤。
B：这是二斤半，行吗？
A：行。

香蕉	三斤	三斤三两
葡萄	四斤	四斤六两
橘子	五斤	五斤二两

二、把下面的词组成句子：

Unscramble the following into normal sentences：

1. 这　简单　很　事

2. 多少　一斤　香蕉　钱

3. 哪儿 买 水果 可以 到

4. 你 不 问 买 价 东西 吗

5. 生意 怎么样 的 你 做 得

三、完成对话：
Complete the following dialogues：

A：你买小贩的东西吗？
B：_____。

A：你买东西的时候，喜欢砍价吗？
B：_____。

A：现在，苹果多少钱一斤？
B：_____。

A：_____？
B：这儿的水果很不错。

A：你喜欢去商店买东西吗？
B：_____。

四、在下列句子中填写"会"与"能"，如能互换，讲讲有什么不同：
Fill in the blanks with 会 or 能. If they are interchangeable, tell their differences if any：

1. 学了三个月汉语,应该_____说一点儿汉语了。

2. 买小贩的东西_____砍价吗?

3. 你_____用汉语打电话吗?

4. 蒙人的事,我们不_____做。

5. 她_____自己开车上班了。

6. 经理是个好人,_____帮助朋友的事,他一定_____帮助。

7. 今天银行不_____兑换钱。

8. 不_____走,怎么_____跑?

五、在下列句子中填写"怎么"与"怎么样":
Fill in the blanks with 怎么 or 怎么样:

1. 经理_____请求,太太也不让他抽烟。
2. 你汉语学得不错,你是_____学习的?
3. _____才能学好汉语?
4. 顾客_____说,服务员也不生气。
5. _____才能不堵车呢?

六、模仿例句说话:
Make sentences according to the example:
例句:不是不会砍价,是不能在这儿砍价

1. 会   能   抽烟

2. 会   能   做生意

3. 会   能   打的

4. 会   能   买东西

5. 会   能   预订房间

七、会话练习：

Situational conversation：

情景：两个顾客，一个小贩；
顾客砍价，小贩蒙人。

Here are two customers and a vendor. The customers are trying to cut the price while the vendor is trying to cheat them.

八、读拼音，写汉字：

Read the following passage and then write it out in Chinese characters：

Jiékè hé Zhēnní qù mǎi píngguǒ. Zhēnní shuō tā huì kǎn jià. Jiékè xiǎng shìshi Zhēnní shìbúshì zhēn de huì kǎn jià, jiù hé tā yìqǐ qù mǎi píngguǒ. Zhēnní kǎn le bàn tiān jià, gāogāoxìngxìng mǎi le sān jīn píngguǒ, kě háishì gěi xiǎofàn mēng le.

第十六课　你会买东西吗(二)
Lesson 16　Do You Know How to Make Purchases (2)

课文
Text

在课外

珍　妮：杰克,你喜欢看广告吗?
杰　克：不喜欢也要看啊!
珍　妮：为什么?
杰　克：不看,怎么买东西?
珍　妮：看了,就会买吗?
杰　克：那当然,不信,我们就试试。
珍　妮：那……我们去买一个西瓜吧!
杰　克：好的。

珍　妮：杰克,你看这小黑板上写的字!
杰　克：一斤一元五角,正宗美国西瓜118,缺点：太甜。
珍　妮：中国卖的美国西瓜,你吃过吗?

杰　克：还没有吃过。
珍　妮：怎么样，买吗？
杰　克：买！这瓜甜，我爱吃。

杰　克：西瓜多少钱一斤？
小　贩：一块五！
杰　克：太贵了！能便宜一点儿吗？
小　贩：不能。这是正宗美国118。
杰　克：你这小黑板上写的不蒙人吧？
小　贩：哪能啊！
杰　克：好，小老板，挑一个！
小　贩：好咧！
杰　克：多少钱？
小　贩：十一斤半，一共十七块两毛五分，给十七块钱吧。
杰　克：开一个口子。
小　贩：好咧！
杰　克：小老板，这瓜怎么一点儿也不甜啊！
小　贩：这儿写着呢，缺点是太甜，优点就是不甜啰！
杰　克：啊！你这广告……
珍　妮：怎么样，杰克？广告也蒙人！

生词
New Words

1. 广告　　　guǎnggào　　advertisement
2. （相）信　（xiāng）xìn　believe

3.	西瓜	xīguā	watermelon
4.	黑板	hēibǎn	blackboard
5.	写	xiě	write
6.	字	zì	word, character
7.	正宗	zhèngzōng	authentic, genuine
8.	缺点	quēdiǎn	shortcoming
9.	甜	tián	sweet
10.	吃	chī	eat
11.	过	guò	(auxiliary indicating that an action or a state was in the past)
12.	贵	guì	expensive
13.	便宜	piányi	cheap
14.	挑(选)	tiāo(xuǎn)	choose, select, pick out
15.	咧	lie	(a dialectal particle)
16.	一共	yīgòng	altogether, in all
17.	口子	kǒuzi	opening, hole, cut, tear
18.	着	zhe	(auxiliary indicating that an action is in progress or a state is continuing)
19.	优点	yōudiǎn	merit, strong point
20.	啰	luo	(particle)

注释
Notes

一、"着"、"了"、"过",时态助词。汉语里的动词,词形本身没有时态变化。动词的时态,是通过助词"着"、"了"、"过"来表示的。

"着",表示动作正在进行或状态正在持续,常跟副词"正"、"在"、"正在"配合使用。例如:

着,了 and 过 are tense auxiliaries. Verbs in Chinese do not have variations in form to indicate the change of tenses. Tenses of verbs are expressed through such auxiliary words as 着,了 and 过.

着 indicates that an action is in progress or a state is continuing. It is often used together with such adverbs as 正,在 or 正在.

1. 他开着车还打电话。
2. 她吃着东西还说个不停。
3. 我们正吃着饭,客人来了。
4. 我们说着说着,她就生气了。

二、"了",表示动作已经完成,可用于实际已经发生的事情的完成,也可用于悬想中将要发生的事情或假设可能发生的事情的完成。例如:

了 indicates that an action is completed, which can either be the completion of an action that has actually occurred, or the completion of an action that one thinks will happen or an action that one presumes may happen.

1. 小王来了,小谢没有来。
2. 等经理来了,我告诉他。
3. 你学会砍价了吗?
4. 我当了大老板,也要感谢你。

三、"过",表示行为或状态已经成为过去,或悬想中已经成为过去。"过"常常与"已经"配合使用。例如:

过 indicates that an action or a state was something in the past, or that one presumes it to be something in the past. 过 is often used together with 已经 (already).

1. 你去过上海吗?
2. 我已经去过上海。
3. 他还没有去过上海。
4. 去年我去过上海,今年我还没有去。
5. 去过上海,就知道上海多么漂亮了。

补充生词
Additional New Words

欺骗　　qīpiàn　　　deceive, cheat

练习
Exercises

一、**替换练习**:
　　Substitution drills:

A：这种西瓜怎么样？
B：我不买。
A：为什么？
B：太甜，我不喜欢。

手机	贵	没钱
苹果	小	不好吃
汽车	便宜	没好货

A：你的优点是什么？
B：喜欢学习。
A：你的缺点是什么？
B：学了就忘。

看书	不爱上班
交朋友	很难理解别人
说话	说话不得体
帮助人	太爱钱

二、把下面的词组成句子：

Unscramble the following into normal sentences：

1. 你 她 相信 应该

2. 广告 事 告诉 多 你 很 可以

3. 便宜 好货 有 也

4. 你 挑 吗 会 西瓜

5. 钱 一共 三斤 多少 苹果

三、完成对话：

Complete the following dialogues：

A：你相信广告吗？
B：＿＿＿＿＿＿＿＿。

A：你为什么喜欢买便宜货？
B：_____。

A：_____？
B：三斤苹果,一斤香蕉,一共是 13.50 元。

A：_____？
B：不能再便宜了。

四、在下列各句中填写"着"、"了"、"过",如果"了"、"过"都可填,讲讲二者的不同:

Fill in the blanks with 着, 了 or 过. If both 了 and 过 can be used, tell their differences if any:

1. 她正挑选____,售货员走来了,说:"我可以帮你吗？"
2. 我给你打____电话,你不在。
3. 你们已经收____我的停车费,怎么还要收？
4. 我学____半年汉语,可是都忘了。
5. 他用自己的钱帮助____很多朋友。
6. 你去____长城吗？
7. 老板喜欢看____价格谈生意。
8. 你在中国坐____出租车吗？
9. 他们正说____什么,我去了,他们就都不说话了。
10. 他用旅行支票兑换____现金。

五、模仿例句说话:

Make sentences according to the example:

例句:我们去买一个便宜点的西瓜吧！

1. 买　　正宗法国葡萄酒

2. 买　　苹果

3. 喝　　橘子汁

4. 坐　　车

5. 听　　课

例句:你看这小黑板上写的字!
1. 服务台　　留的

2. 广告　　介绍的

3. 矿泉水瓶　写的

4. 约会时　　说的

5. 发票上　　写的

例句:这瓜怎么一点儿也不甜啊!
1. 东西　　　便宜

2. 这儿　　　好玩

3. 苹果　　　好吃

4. 黑板上写的字　明白

六、用你学过的词语写出一则推销水果的广告。

Write an ad to push the sales of fruits.

七、会话练习：

Situational conversations：

情景1：买水果，你要挑，小老板不让你挑：

You are buying things (fruit). You want to pick and choose and the vender doesn't allow you to.

情景2：买水果，小老板让你挑，你不会挑：

You are buying things (fruit). You are allowed to pick and choose but you don't know how.

情景3：买水果，小老板少称了，你回去怎么找小老板：

The vendor gave you short weight. How are you going to make the complaint?

八、读拼音，写汉字：

Read the following passage, and then write it out in Chinese characters：

Mài xīguā de xiǎofàn zài xiǎo hēibǎn shang xiě zhe: zhèngzōng Měiguó xīguā 118, quēdiǎn: tài tián. Zhè shì shénme yìsi ne? Shì shuō tā mài de xīguā tài tián, zhè shì yī ge quēdiǎn, háishì shuō xīguā tài tián, shì yīge quēdiǎn, tā de xīguā méiyǒu zhè ge quēdiǎn, yī diǎnr yě bù tián. Jiékè shì zěnme lǐjiě de ne? Tā lǐjiě de duì ma?

157

第十七课 她怎么了(一)
Lesson 17　What's the Matter with Her (1)

课文
Text

在课内

王老师：同学们，早上好！
学　生：老师早上好！
王老师：同学们都来了吗？
珍　妮：安娜和杰克没有来。
王老师：他们怎么了？
珍　妮：安娜病了，杰克陪她去医院了。
王老师：什么病？
珍　妮：可能是感冒了，她说很不舒服。
王老师：发烧吗？量体温没有？
珍　妮：量了。38.5℃。
王老师：啊，烧得不低。咳嗽吗？
珍　妮：不咳嗽，嗓子也不疼，可总叫口渴。

王老师:应该多喝水。
珍　妮:那可不行!她拉肚子。
王老师:拉肚子就更得多喝水。
珍　妮:那不更要拉肚子了吗?
王老师:哦,不会的。
山　口:我想,她不一定是感冒了,很可能是吃坏了肚子。
王老师:现在上课吧,下课以后,我们去看看她。

生词
New Words

1. 病　　bìng　　　ill, sick, disease
2. 陪　　péi　　　 accompany
3. 医院　yīyuàn　　hospital
4. 可能　kěnéng　　possible, probable, likely, maybe
5. 感冒　gǎnmào　　common cold
6. 舒服　shūfu　　 be well, comfortable
7. 发烧　fāshāo　　run a fever, have a temperature
8. 量　　liáng　　　measure
9. 体温　tǐwēn　　 (body) temperature
10. 度　　dù　　　　degree
11. 摄氏　shèshì　　centigrade, celsius
12. 低　　dī　　　　low
13. 咳嗽　késou　　 cough
14. 嗓子　sǎngzi　　throat, larynx, voice
15. 疼　　téng　　　ache, pain, sore

16.	口	kǒu	mouth, opening
17.	渴	kě	thirsty
18.	水	shuǐ	water
19.	拉	lā	pull, drag; empty the bowels
20.	肚子	dùzi	belly, abdomen, stomach
21.	更	gèng	still more, even more, further
22.	坏	huài	bad, harmful
23.	上课	shàngkè	attend class, conduct a class
24.	下课	xiàkè	finish class, after class

注释
Notes

一、"可"、"可是",连词。说话人先提出一个肯定的事实,然后用"可"或"可是"作转折,引出与前面相反的意思,说话人强调的是后一层意思。例如:

可 and 可是 are conjunctions. The speaker first mentions a certain fact, and then uses 可 or 可是 as a turn to introduce a statement contrary to the above mentioned fact. What the speaker stresses is the latter.

1. 我想你不会来,可你还是来了。
2. 这话是你说的,我可没那么说。
3. 他是个什么样的人,你不知道,可我知道。
4. 我已经是大人了,可爸爸、妈妈还当我是个孩子。

"可",也是副词,表示强调,重读时还有夸张的意味。例如:

可 is also an adverb, indicating emphasis. When it is stressed, it implies exaggeration.

1. 你可真坏!
2. 这事儿真可气!
3. 你可不能这样做!
4. 他可是一个好人!
5. 商店的人可多啦!

"可"用在感叹盼望的事情或某种愿望已经实现时,有"终于"的意思。例如:
When 可 is used in exclamation to express realization of an expected thing or a certain wish, it has the implication of "eventually".

1. 离家三年了,今天可回家了!
2. 大家等你半天了,你可来了!
3. 今天,我可找到工作啦!
4. 哈,这下我可有钱了!

二、"可能",副词,表示估计。多数副词不能单独回答问题,例如"很"、"太"、"更"、"又"等等,而副词"可能"可以。例如:
可能 is an adverb expressing an estimation. While most adverbs cannot be used alone to answer questions, 可能 can be used in this way.

1. 他可能没有上班。
2. 他没有钱,他爸爸可能有钱。
3. 这种车可能很贵。

4. 这花儿她会喜欢吗？
可能吧。

三、"更",副词,用作比较,表示程度高,有进一步加深的意思。在句子中常常列举出比较的两个方面。例如：

更, as an adverb, is used in comparison to indicate a high degree, with the implication of further deepening. Both of the two sides of comparison are often given in the sentence.

1. 最近几年,北京更漂亮了。
2. 这个咖啡厅的顾客多了,东西也更贵了。
3. 她去年就学得不错,今年就学得更好了。
4. 他爱爸爸,可更爱妈妈。

"更"还可用于比较几种事物,表示几种事物中某种事物最突出,最值得特别提出来。例如：

更 can also be used for the comparison of several things, indicating that among those things one of them is most outstanding and worth mentioning.

1. 她不喝酒,不抽烟,更不吸毒(xīdú take drugs)。
2. 他不会忘了同学、同事、朋友,更不会忘了老师。
3. 小王想当老师,也想当医生,可更想当公司大老板。

补充生词
Additional New Words

华氏　　Huáshì　　　　Fahrenheit

| 请假 | qǐngjià | ask for leave |
| 迟到 | chídào | be late |

练习
Exercises

一、替换练习:

Substitution drills:

A:你怎么了?
B:我有点儿不舒服。

| 嗓子痛 |
| 发烧 |
| 拉肚子 |

A:你量过体温吗?
B:量过了。
A:多少度?
B:36.5℃。
A:你不发烧。

37℃	不烧
37.5℃	有点儿低烧
40.6℃	烧得不低

A:谁陪安娜去医院了?
B:杰克陪安娜去医院了。

谢文	邮局	小王
朱丽亚	买西瓜	马克
山口	老师办公室	珍妮
杰克妈妈	旅行	杰克的中国朋友

二、把下面的词组成句子:

Unscramble the following into normal sentences:

1. 我 你 陪 打 去 电话

2. 今天 来 谁 没 上课

3. 我 已经 感冒 了 好 的

4. 别 肚子 坏 吃 了

5. 我们 看看 去 她 吧

三、完成对话：

Complete the following dialogues：

A：他今天为什么又请假了？
B：＿＿＿＿＿＿＿＿＿＿＿＿＿。

A：你在中国学汉语，上课迟到吗？
B：＿＿＿＿＿＿＿＿＿＿＿＿＿。

A：你要是感冒了，去医院吗？
B：＿＿＿＿＿＿＿＿＿＿＿＿＿。

A：发烧时你喝水还是喝茶？
B：＿＿＿＿＿＿＿＿＿＿＿＿＿。

四、下列各句中的"可"语法意思不同，请指出它的不同意思：

Point out the different meanings of 可 in the following sentences：

1. 你这么说,她可真要生气了。

2. 喝了酒可不能开车。

3. 他汉语说得可好了。

4. 老师病了,可是还给我们上课。

5. 他喝了很多水,可还是口渴。

6. 要学好汉语可不容易。

五、下列各句中"更"的语法意思不同,请指出它的不同意思:

Point out the different meanings of 更 in the following sentences:

1. 他更有钱了。

2. 他抽烟后嗓子更疼了。

3. 经理喜欢喝咖啡,也喜欢喝啤酒,更喜欢喝中国茶。

4. 公司去年生意好,今年生意更好。

5. 他想当老板,更相当大老板。

六、模仿例句说话:

Make sentences according to the example:

例句：她不一定是感冒，很可能是吃坏了肚子。
1. 有事　　　病了

2. 去医院　　回家了

3. 不想买　　没有钱

4. 不想帮助你　不能帮助你

例句：拉肚子就更得多喝水
1. 说不好　　多练习

2. 发烧　　　多喝水

3. 不会挑水果　多问

4. 做生意　　有朋友

5. 请别人帮助　有礼貌

七、会话练习：

Situational conversation：

情景：学生不能上课，向老师请假。说明为什么？
A student cannot come to class. He wants to ask for the teacher's leave, and is explaining his reason.

八、读拼音，写汉字：

Read the following passage and then write it out in Chinese characters:

Yītiān, lǎoshī shàngkè de shíhou, wèn tóngxuémen shìbushì dōu lái le. Shānkǒu shuō Ānnà méiyǒu lái, kěshì yě méiyǒu qǐngjià. Lǎoshī wèn tā wèishénme bù lái shàngkè. Zhēnní shuō Ānnà bìng le, kěnéng shì gǎnmào le, kě Shānkǒu shuō, bù yīdìng shì gǎnmào, hěn kěnéng shì chī huài le dùzi. Lǎoshī shuō, xiàkè yǐhòu, wǒmen dàjiā yīqǐ qù kànkan Ānnà.

第十八课　她怎么了（二）
Lesson 18　What's the Matter with Her（2）

课文
Text

在课外

钱富成：先生，你们是去旅行吗？
杰　克：是啊。你呢？
钱富成：出差，跑买卖。
杰　克：做生意？怎么不坐飞机？
钱富成：吃点苦，节省点经费。
杰　克：可火车太慢。生意人最讲究的就是时间。
钱富成：是啊。时间就是金钱嘛！
杰　克：可是……
钱富成：没关系，今天是休息日。
杰　克：对了，大家都不上班。
钱富成：你的朋友怎么一路都在睡觉？

杰　　克：她病了几天了，叫她别来，可她一定要来。
钱富成：怎么光睡觉，不吃点药？
杰　　克：忘了带了，想下了火车去买。
钱富成：啊，你们等等，我去找大夫。

钱富成：大夫来了。
大　　夫：小姐怎么了？
安　　娜：前几天拉肚子，现在不拉了，可头疼得厉害。
大　　夫：哦，你正在发高烧呢，量一量体温吧。
安　　娜：大夫，我得了什么病？
大　　夫：把体温表给我。40℃，烧得厉害。让我看看嗓子。
杰　　克：有什么问题吗？
大　　夫：嗓子发炎了。
杰　　克：要打针吗？她怕打针！
大　　夫：先吃点退烧药吧。一次吃两片，四小时吃一次。
安　　娜：大夫，我的病要紧吗？
大　　夫：下了车，去医院好好检查检查吧。
安　　娜：啊，上帝，可别住院！

生词
New Words

1.	出差	chūchāi	go on a business trip, travel on official business
2.	飞机	fēijī	aircraft, plane
3.	火车	huǒchē	train

4.	苦	kǔ	bitter, hardship, cause sb. suffering
5.	节省	jiéshěng	economize, save, use sparingly
6.	经费	jīngfèi	funds, outlay
7.	慢	màn	slow
8.	讲究	jiǎngjiu	stress, be particular about; pay attention to
9.	时间	shíjiān	time
10.	金钱	jīnqián	money
11.	嘛	ma	(particle indicating that something is obvious)
12.	休息	xiūxi	rest
13.	一路	yīlù	all the way, throughout the journey; of the same kind
14.	睡觉	shuìjiào	sleep
15.	光	guāng	only, alone; light
16.	药	yào	medicine
17.	带	dài	take, bring, carry
18.	大夫	dàifu	doctor
19.	体温表	tǐwēnbiǎo	thermometer
20.	厉害	lìhai	severe, terrible, harsh
21.	发炎	fāyán	inflammation
22.	怕	pà	fear, be afraid of
23.	打针	dǎzhēn	give or have an injection
24.	退	tuì	move back, decline, fade, give back

25. 片	piàn	tablet, slice
26. 要紧	yàojǐn	serious, important
27. 检查	jiǎnchá	check up, inspect, examine
28. 上帝	shàngdì	God
29. 住院	zhùyuàn	be hospitalized

专名
Proper Noun

钱富成　Qián Fùchéng　Qian Fucheng

注释
Notes

一、"时间"与"时候",都是名词,表示有起点、有终点的一段时间,也可表示时间里的某一点。但是这两个词,也有一点区别。"时候",多用于口语;"时间"用于口语,多用来说明时间点和较确定的、具体的时间。在书面语体中,表达时间概念时,不适宜用"时候",而要用"时间"。"时候"还可以说"当……的时候",而"时间"不这么说。例如:

Both 时间 and 时候 are nouns indicating a duration of time with a starting point and an ending point. They can also express a point of time. However, there is a little difference between these two words. 时候 is more frequently used in spoken Chinese. When 时间 is used in spoken Chinese, it more often than not expresses a point of time or a definite or concrete time. In written Chinese, we should use 时间 rather than 时候 to express the concept of time. We can also say：当……的时候, but 时间 cannot be used in this way.

    1. 你今天用了多少时间做练习？
    2. 火车什么时候到北京？
    3. 火车到北京的时间是十二点零五分。
    4. 她小时候是个很漂亮的女孩儿。
    5. 当他想起爸爸妈妈的时候，他就想回家。
    6. 时间在一分一秒地过去，还是不知道飞机哪儿出了问题。

二、"把"，作介词时，构成"把"字句，是现代汉语里常用的句式，也是外国人较难掌握的句型，需要特别注意学习。"把"字句中的主要动词一般都是及物动词，是能支配后面的宾语的。"把"字后的名词是这个主要动词的宾语，用"把"字提到动词的前面去了。动词后还应有相关成分，不能只剩下一个单独的动词。例如，不能说"把门关"，要说"把门关上"。充当宾语的名词，所指事物必须是确定的，已知的。例如：

把，when used as a preposition, constructs a 把-sentence, which is a common sentence pattern in modern Chinese, and which is difficult for foreigners to master. Hence it deserves special attention. The main verb in the 把-sentence is generally a transitive verb, which can govern the object that follows it. The noun after the character 把 is the object of this main verb, and 把 brings it forward to a place before the verb. The verb cannot stand alone either, that is, there must be some related elements after it. For instance, for "close the door", we cannot say 把门关, but have to say 把门关上. The referent of the noun functioning as the object must be something definite, something that is already known。

> 1. 请你把这本书给他。——请你给他这本书。
> 2. 我把药吃下去了。——我吃了药了。
> 3. 他把"四"念成(niàn chéng)"十"了——"四"他念成"十"了。
> 4. 你把我忘了——你忘了我了。
> 5. 我把练习做完了——我做完练习了。
> 6. 我把肚子吃坏了——我吃坏肚子了。

补充生词
Additional New Words

快	kuài	fast, quick, soon
双休日	shuāngxiūrì	two days for rest

练习
Exercises

一、**替换练习**:

Substitution drills:

A:你们是去<u>旅行</u>吗?
B:不,我们是去<u>出差</u>。

火车站	飞机场
北京大学	经贸大学
找朋友	看大夫
买药	打针

A:你的头疼厉害吗？
B:很厉害,疼得睡不着觉。

感冒	十几天高烧不退
护士	她天天要我打针吃药
医生	他不让我出院
老板	他不再给我工作

二、把下面的词组成句子：

Unscramble the following into normal sentences：

1. 你　出差　哪儿　去

2. 她　能　吃苦　不

3. 你　钱　应该　花　节省　点儿

4. 坐　帮助　能　中国　火车　了解　我

5. 我　要紧　有事　走　了　得

三、完成对话：

Complete the following dialogues：

A:你去旅行的时候生过病吗？
B:_____。

A:_____？
B:我怕打针。

A:你昨天晚上睡得怎么样？
B:_____。

A：你带钱了吗？
B：对不起，_____。

A：_____？
B：我在家休息。

四、在下列各句中填写"时间"、"时候"，并想想为什么：
Fill in the blanks with 时间 or 时候：

1. 生病的_____最想家。
2. 要是你想学习就会有_____。
3. 有钱的_____不要忘了没钱的朋友。
4. 坐飞机可以省_____，可没有坐火车有意思。
5. 请别人帮助的_____，应该有礼貌。
6. _____不多了，可考试我还没准备好。
7. 开车的_____不能打电话。
8. 上课的_____好好上课，下课的_____好好休息，这才是会学习的好学生。

五、把下列各句改成"把"字句：
Rewrite the following sentences into 把-sentences：

1. 请系好安全带。

2. 你这个字写错了。

3. 你忘了她吧。

4. 请你给我体温表。

5. 这杯酒我已经喝完了。

把"把"字句改成不带"把"字的陈述句：
Rewrite the following 把-sentences into narrative sentences without 把：

1. 我把她送回家了。

2. 我把发票给了顾客了。

3. 哥哥把这本书看完了。

4. 秘书把工作安排好了。

5. 我把给妈妈留言的事忘了。

六、模仿例句说话：
Make sentences according to the example：

例句：生意人最讲究的就是时间。

生病	最苦的	就是
旅行	最怕的	就是
学汉语	最要紧的	就是
老师	最喜欢的	就是

七、会话练习：

Situational conversation：

情景：陪生病的朋友去医院看病，大夫问病、检查，你或朋友回答。

Accompany your sick friend to see the doctor. The doctor inquires about the symptoms and gives your friend a check-up, you or your friend answers the doctor's questions.

八、读拼音，写汉字：

Read the following passage and then write it out in Chinese characters：

Qián jīnglǐ chūchāi, zài huǒchē shàng rènshi le liúxué shēng Jiékè hé Ānnà. Tāmen yīlù shàng shuō le hěn duō huà. Jiékè bù lǐjiě, Qián jīnglǐ chūchāi zuò shēngyi, wèi shénme bù zuò fēijī. Qián jīnglǐ shuō, zhè liǎng tiān shì shuāng xiū rì, dàjiā dōu bù shàngbān, zuò huǒchē, bù huì wùshì, hái kěyǐ jiéshěng jīngfèi.

第十九课　是谁的错（一）
Lesson 19　Whose Fault Is It（1）

课文
Text

在课内

杰　　克：老师，你好！
王老师：你好！今天你怎么又迟到了？
杰　　克：我没迟到呀！看，我的手表现在才七点五十分。我还早到了呢！
珍　　妮：才七点五十分？都八点过一刻了！晚了一刻钟了！
杰　　克：怎么会？一定是你的表错了。
王老师：好了，坐下吧，把书拿出来。

杰　　克：哎呀，糟糕了！
珍　　妮：你又拿错书了，是不是？
杰　　克：不是张老师的听力课吗？怎么是王老师上课？

珍　妮:这节课是王老师的口语课!
杰　克:我刚才走进教室就觉得奇怪!今天星期几?
珍　妮:今天星期二!
杰　克:星期二?看,我的手表是星期一。
珍　妮:我说你昨天怎么没来上课呢,原来昨天是你的星期天啊!
杰　克:我可没休息,我打工赚钱去了!

王老师:你们俩在说什么呢?
珍　妮:杰克以为今天是星期一,所以他只带了听力课本。
杰　克:老师,这不能怪我,是表错了。我保证,明天它不会再错了。
山　口:如果明天你上课再迟到,又该怪谁呢?
杰　克:是啊,又该怪谁呢?怪我自己?哦,不……

生词
New Words

1. 迟到　chídào　be late
2. 手表　shǒubiǎo　wrist watch
3. 早　zǎo　early; morning; long ago
4. 晚　wǎn　late; evening, night
5. 拿　ná　hold, take
6. 出来　chūlai　(used after a verb indicating motion out towards the

			speaker, completion of an action, or revealing, etc.)
7.	哎呀	āiyā	(interjection expressing surprise or complaint)
8.	糟糕	zāogāo	too bad, how terrible
9.	听力	tīnglì	listening comprehension, hearing
10.	口语	kǒuyǔ	spoken language, oral (class)
11.	节	jié	period, joint, section
12.	觉得	jué de	feel, think
13.	奇怪	qíguài	strange, odd
14.	原来	yuánlái	original; actually; as it turns out
15.	打工	dǎgōng	do mannal work; work as an employee
16.	赚钱	zhuànqián	earn money, make a profit
17.	俩	liǎ	two
18.	以为	yǐwéi	think, believe, consider
19.	所以	suǒyǐ	as a result, therefore
20.	课本	kèběn	textbook
21.	怪	guài	blame, strange
22.	如果	rúguǒ	if, in case
23.	保证	bǎozhèng	pledge, guarantee, ensure
24.	它	tā	it

注释
Notes

一、"才",副词,表示事情发生或结束得晚。例如:
才, adverb, expresses that something happens or ends late.

  1. 你怎么才来教室?
  2. 你为什么现在才说呢?
  3. 他喝了三杯开水,才把药吃下去。

"才",也表示事情在不久前发生。例如:
才 also expresses that something happened not long ago.

  1. 我们才上课。
  2. 我们才学了生词。
  3. 我昨天才认识他。
  4. 小王才工作三年。

二、"都",副词,表示总括全部。例如:
都, adverb, expresses that all are included.

  1. 我们都来了。
  2. 我们互相都认识。
  3. 我们都学习汉语。

"都……了",强调时间迫近或情况早已存在。"都"要轻读,重音在"都"的后边。例如:
都…了 emphasizes that the time is drawing near or the

situation has long existed. Here 都 should be pronounced softly, with the stress fallen on what comes after 都.

1. 快跑,火车都进站了。
2. 他都生气了,你还说个不停!
3. 我们约好九点钟见面,都十点了,他还不来。
4. 她都快工作了,还像一个小孩儿。

三、"我说……呢"或者"我说呢",表示忽然醒悟、明白。后面常用"原来"带出所"醒悟"到的是什么。例如:

我说……呢 or 我说呢 expresses a sudden realization or understanding. It is often followed by 原来 to introduce what it is that has been understood.

1. 我说你怎么会拉肚子呢,原来是你吃多了羊肉串!
2. 我说呢,他怎么来晚了,原来是表坏了。
3. 我说呢,他的口语这么好,原来他有很多中国朋友。

四、"原来",副词,表示说话人发现了以前不知道的情况,或对某种情况有所醒悟。例如:

原来, as an adverb, indicates that the speaker has discovered something he didn't know before, or that he has come to realize something.

1. 我说是谁呢,原来是你啊!
2. 我以为你知道呢,原来你也不知道。
3. 他出门就叫出租车,原来他打工赚了很多钱。
4. 大家都奇怪他今天为什么没来上班,原来是病了。

五、"如果",表示假设,用在前一分句,有时后面还可加助词"的话";后一分句常与"就、也、那么"等词相呼应,表示在前一种假设情况下出现的结果。例如:

如果 (if) expresses a supposition. It is used in the first clause. Sometimes it can be followed by 的话. The second clause often echoes with such words as 就 (then), 也 (too) or 那么 (then), expressing an outcome resulting from that supposition.

1. 如果你去(的话),我也去。
2. 如果便宜(的话),我就买。
3. 你如果相信他,那可就糟糕了!
4. 如果你觉得那样做不好,就不要那样做。

六、"所以",连词,用来表示因果关系,或推理和结论的关系。例如:

所以, as a conjunction, expresses a cause-effect relationship, or a reasoning-conclusion relationship.

1. 我没有工作,所以我没有钱。
2. 我得到老师很多帮助,所以我的汉语学得很好。
3. 他太容易相信人,所以他常常吃苦头。
4. 我不了解她,所以我不知道她以后想做什么。

补充生词
Additional New Words

站	zhàn	station; stand
见面	jiànmiàn	meet, see

羊肉串　yángròu chuànr　mutton cubes roasted on a skewer

练习
Exercises

一、**替换练习**：

Substitution drills：

A：哎呀，糟了！
B：你怎么了？
A：我拿错书了。
B：真的？以后可别再拿错书了！

看	表
吃	药
认	人
叫	名字

A：你今天不是有课吗？怎么还睡觉？
B：我好像有点不舒服。

休息	上班来了
一个人在家没意思	
要出差	一点也没准备
有了新的安排	
有约会	没买鲜花
已经取消了约会	
要去看女朋友	不早点儿走
想试试她会不会等我	

二、把下面的词组成句子：

Unscramble the following into normal sentences：

1. 上课　迟到　你　了

2. 没有　今天　我们　口语课

3. 我们　哪儿　听力课　在　上

4. 你　才　怎么　呢　现在　来

5. 我　没有　保证　他　你　忘记

三、完成对话：

Complete the following dialogues：

A：_____？
B：不会迟到,现在还早呢,才七点四十五分！
A：你的表不会错吧？
B：_____。

A：喂,谁拿了我的书？
B：_____吧？
A：我问小王了,他说他没拿我的书。
B：_____。

A：经理,对不起,我昨天没有来上班。
B：_____？
A：_____。
B：我说呢,原来是病了。

A：在贵国,你打工挣钱吗？

B：_____。
A：_____？_____？
B：在饭店当服务员一个小时五美元。

四、区别下列各句中"才"的不同含义：

Distinguish the different meanings of 才 in the following sentences：

1. 我们才认识。
2. 他发烧三天了才去医院。
3. 我真不相信,他才学了一年汉语就说得这么好。
4. 他打了三天针才不拉肚子。
5. 他昨天工作到早上2点才睡觉。

五、读出下列各句的重音,说明各句中"都"字的含义：

Read the following sentences and get the stresses right. Then explain the meaning of 都 in these sentences：

1. 大家都以为你不来了,你怎么又来了？
2. 没问题了,钱都兑换好了。
3. 你都发烧了,还不吃药。
4. 大家都觉得奇怪,老板怎么什么都知道了。
5. 去中国旅行要带什么,我都告诉他了。
6. 都打工挣钱了,还说没钱请朋友喝啤酒。
7. 都什么时候了,还在睡觉？

六、用"我说……呢,原来……"句型说话：

Make sentences according to the example：

例句：我说你昨天怎么没来上课呢，原来昨天是你的星期天啊！

    1. 现在有钱了　　　　打工挣钱

    2. 了解她　　　　　　你们是朋友

    3. 送鲜花给她　　　　她的生日

    4. 还睡觉　　　　　　病了

    5. 高兴　　　　　　　妈妈来了

用"如果……就……"句型说话：
Make sentences using the pattern 如果…就：

例句：如果你明天再迟到，以后就别来上班了。

    1. 有时间　　　　　　去看你

    2. 不舒服　　　　　　看医生

    3. 路上堵车　　　　　糟糕了

    4. 相信我　　　　　　交朋友

    5. 有钱　　　　　　　帮助她们

七、**会话练习：**

    Situational conversation：

情景：去约会的时候，你向对方解释为什么去晚了。
Explain why you are late for the appointment.

八、读拼音，写汉字：

Read the following passage, and then write it out in Chinese characters:

  Jiékè shàngkè, chángcháng chídào, hái chángcháng ná cuò shū. Wèi shénme? Jiékè zǒngshì shuō, shì tā de shǒubiǎo bù hǎo. Tā shàngkè chídào hé ná cuò shū, bù néng guài tā, yīnggāi guài shǒubiǎo. Jiékè wèi shénme zhème xiǎng ne? Zhēn qíguài!

第二十课 是谁的错(二)
Lesson 20 Whose Fault Is It (2)

课文
Text

在课外

杰 克:小姐,从上海来的14次特别快车什么时候到?

小 姐:九点零一分到站。现在才七点半,还早呢!

杰 克:什么?才七点半?

小 姐:是呀,你看,这大楼上的钟,不是七点半吗?

杰 克:不对!我刚对过表,现在是八点半,一定是大楼上的钟慢了。

小 姐:那怎么会?是你的表快了。

杰 克:是吗?这该死的表,害得我这么早就起床,现在还得等一个多小时。

小 姐:你是来接人的?

杰　　克：是，接上海来的一个朋友。
小　　姐：你的朋友是第一次来北京？
杰　　克：不，他常坐火车来北京出差，我是第一次来火车站。
小　　姐：哦，这么说，你的朋友应该来接你。
杰　　克：为什么？
小　　姐：他不会说，这大楼上的钟错了！

杰　　克：喂，史特凡，我在这儿！
史特凡：嗨，杰克，见到你真高兴！
杰　　克：一路顺利吧？
史特凡：一切顺利！
杰　　克：你总是一切顺利，我可是常常遇到麻烦。
史特凡：怎么啦？
杰　　克：这该死的表，总耽误事儿！
史特凡：你的表怎么了？
杰　　克：前几天太慢，我上课总迟到；今天又太快，害得我在这儿等了你一个多小时！
史特凡：哈……你要是我公司的职员，我一定要开除你！

生词
New Words

1. 从　　　cóng　　from; follow, obey
2. 特别　　tèbié　　special
3. 快　　　kuài　　fast, quick

4.	楼	lóu	a storeyed building, storey, floor
5.	死	sǐ	die, be dead; extremely; rigid
6.	害	hài	cause trouble to, harm, murdur
7.	这么	zhème	so, such; this way, like this
8.	起床	qǐchuáng	get up, get out of bed
9.	接	jiē	meet, welcome, connect, receive
10.	第	dì	(used before numerals to form ordinal numbers)
11.	顺利	shùnlì	smooth, without a hitch
12.	一切	yīqiè	all, every, everything
13.	总是	zǒngshì	always, after all
14.	常	cháng	often, frequently
15.	遇到	yùdào	run into, encounter, come across
16.	麻烦	máfan	trouble; inconvenient
17.	耽误	dānwu	delay, hold up
18.	要是	yàoshi	if, suppose, in case
19.	职员	zhíyuán	staff member
20.	开除	kāichú	expel, discharge

专名
Proper Noun

| 史特凡 | Shǐ tè fán | Steven |

注释
Notes

一、"从",作介词,表示起点。例如:
从(from), preposition, indicates the starting point.

    1. 你从哪儿来?
    2. 我从美国来。
    3. 我们从八点开始上课。
    4. 从学校到北京火车站,坐出租车要半个小时。

二、"这么",代词,指称事物的具体性状、程度,或动作的具体方式。事物的这种具体性状、程度,或动作的具体方式,是说话人和听话人都了解的。例如:
这么, pronoun, refers to the concrete character or degree of something, or the mode of action, which is known by the speaker and hearer.

    1. 你怎么交了这么一个朋友!
    2. 你买了这么个西瓜,真糟糕!
    3. 这事儿不能这么办!
    4. 你这么说,我就明白了。
    5. 他这么爱你,你还不高兴?

三、"总"、"总是",副词,表示过去经常这样,很少例外,现在也还是这样。例如:
总 and 总是 are adverbs indicating that it was always like this in the past, with very few exceptions, and it remains like

this now.

1. 他总缺钱用。
2. 他总是说假话。
3. 他总是找我的麻烦。
4. 你总这样厉害,谁还跟你说真话。

四、"要是",连词,表示假设,意思和"如果"差不多,常与"就"相呼应,多用于口语。"要是……的话"是口语里常用的格式,与"要是"的用法相同,只是语气略强一点。"要是"、"要是……的话"的否定形式是"要不是"。例如:

要是, conjunction, expresses an assumption, whose meaning is similar to 如果. It often corresponds with 就, and is more often than not used orally. 要是…的话 is a formula which is often used in conversation, whose usage is the same as 要是, but with a slightly stronger tone. The negative form for both 要是 and 要是…的话 is 要不是.

1. 要是没有钱,我就不能来中国学习汉语。
2. 我要是不认识她,怎么能了解她。
3. 你要是不想去,你就不要去。
4. 你要是不喜欢的话,就把它送人好了。
5. 他要是我们公司的职员,那才奇怪呢!
6. 要不是该死的手表太快,我才不会这么早起床呢!

"要",也可以作连词,表假设,只是不能像"要是",可以放在主语前边。它只能放在主语后边。例如:

要 can also be used as conjunction, indicating supposition. But unlike 要是, 要 can't occur before the subject. For example:

1. 你要不喜欢，就别买。(不能说"要我不喜欢，就别买")
2. 你要不说，我怎么知道？
3. 你要不会，我可以帮助你。
4. 火车要晚点，可就糟糕了。

补充生词
Additional New Words

| 晚点 | wǎndiǎn | late, behind schedule |
| 正点 | zhèngdiǎn | on time, on schedule |

练习
Exercises

一、替换练习：

Substitution drills：

A：从<u>上海</u>来的<u>14</u>次特别快车什么时候到？
B：<u>九点零一分</u>到站。

西安	280 次快车	20:25
山海关	551 次慢车	14:05
巴黎	CA950 班机	11:45
纽约	班机	22:20

A：你是什么时候<u>来北京</u>的？
B：我是<u>今年9月3日来北京</u>的。
A：你这是第一次<u>来北京</u>吗？
B：不，我这是第二次<u>来北京</u>。

来中国	去年 2 月 25 日
去上海	1993 年 7 月 30 日
去西安	1985 年 10 月 1 日
去巴黎	1995 年 5 月 10 日

A:你是来机场接人的吗?
B:是,我来接留学生。
   你也是来接人的?
A:不,我来送留学生。

朋友	老板
老板	同事
同事	我妈妈
公司总裁	一个朋友

二、把下面的词组成句子:

Unscramble the following into normal sentences:

1. 预订 我 特别快车 14次 一张 要 票

2. 我 机场 接 去 朋友

3. 他 坐 出差 喜欢 火车

4. 这 飞机 误点 了 班

5. 常常 我 麻烦 遇到

三、完成对话:

Complete the following dialogues:

A:你第一次来北京是什么时候?
B:_____。

A:总是迟到的职员,公司会开除他吗?
B:_____。

A:老板,_____?
B:你总是给公司带来麻烦,所以我要开除你。

A:你的生意做得顺利吗？
B:不,_____。

四、模仿例句说话:

Make sentences according to the example:

例句:这该死的表,总是耽误事儿!

1. 电话　　　占线

2. 汽车　　　慢吞吞

3. 马路　　　堵车

4. 司机　　　迟到

5. 小贩　　　蒙人

6. 老板　　　不让我休息

例句:你总是一切顺利,我可是常常遇到麻烦。

1. 好　　　　不好

2. 有钱　　　缺钱

3. 美差　　　苦差

4. 赚钱　　　赔钱

5. 帮助别人　　要别人帮助

6. 出门就打的　　走路

五、用括号里的词完成句子：

Complete the following sentences with the words in the brackets：

1. 我做生意_____。（麻烦）
2. 要是火车晚点，_____。（糟糕）
3. 你到飞机场后，_____。（接）
4. 我很高兴听说，_____。（顺利）
5. 你要是遇到麻烦，_____。（打电话）
6. 你要是找他的麻烦，_____。（生气）

六、会话练习：

Situational conversation：

情景：去飞机场接朋友，可路上堵车。你到机场的时候，飞机早已到了，你向朋友解释，请朋友原谅。

You go to the airport to meet a friend. Because of traffic jam, the plane arrives long before you get to the airport. You apologize to your friend.

七、读拼音，写汉字：

Read the following passage, and then write it out in Chinese characters：

Yītiān, Jiékè qù huǒchēzhàn jiē péngyou. Tā de péngyou zài Shànghǎi zuò shēngyi, chángcháng lái Běijīng chūchāi. Cóng Shànghǎi lái de huǒchē zhèngdiǎn dào le Běijīng zhàn. Jiékè jiàn dào lǎo péngyou, tèbié gāoxìng, tā hěn kuài jiù wàng le tā yù dào de máfan.

第二十一课　住在哪儿（一）
Lesson 21 Where Are You Staying (1)

课文
Text

在课内

王老师：杰克，你住在哪儿？
杰　克：我住在学校的四号楼。
王老师：珍妮，你呢？
珍　妮：我也住在四号楼。
王老师：住几号房间？
珍　妮：3层347，杰克住2层215。
王老师：你们房间里边有电话吗？
杰　克：没有。楼道里有公用电话。
山　口：哦，这不方便。
珍　妮：可不是。我离电话远，常常听不见电话响。
杰　克：有时候，打电话的人太多，还得等好半天。

珍　妮:还是山口好,自己家有电话。

王老师:山口,你住哪儿?
山　口:我住亚运村附近,离学校很近。
王老师:为什么不住学校里边?
杰　克:住学校外边,房租多贵呀!
山　口:我先生的公司给我们租了一套公寓,我们不付房租。
杰　克:环境怎么样?
山　口:很好。购物,娱乐,都很方便。
珍　妮:啊,那真不错!
山　口:欢迎你们去玩。这是我先生的名片,上面有地址和电话号码。
珍　妮:谢谢,有空儿,我们一定去拜访你们。

生词
New Words

1. 里　　lǐ　　　　in, inside
2. 楼道　lóudào　　corridor, passageway
3. 公用　gōngyòng　public; for public use
4. 方便　fāngbiàn　convenient
5. 离　　lí　　　　from; leave
6. 远　　yuǎn　　　far away, distant
7. 响　　xiǎng　　 sound, noise; ring
8. 附近　fùjìn　　 nearby, close to

9.	近	jìn	near, close
10.	里边	lǐbian	inside; within
11.	外边	wàibian	outside
12.	房租	fángzū	rent
13.	套	tào	suite, suit, set, cover
14.	公寓	gōngyù	apartment house, block of flats
15.	付	fù	pay, hand over to
16.	环境	huánjìng	environment
17.	娱乐	yúlè	recreation, amusement
18.	名片	míngpiàn	visiting card
19.	上面	shàngmiàn	on the surface of, above
20.	地址	dìzhǐ	address
21.	有空	yǒukòng	have time to spar
22.	拜访	bàifǎng	pay a visit, call on

专名

Proper Noun

亚运村　　Yàyùncūn　　Asian Games Village

注释

Notes

一、"里、外、上、下、左、右、前、后",是表方位的名词,可以单独使用,也可以用"边"、"面"等词合起来用。例如:

　　里(in),外(out),上(up),下(down),左(left),右(right),

前(in front),后(behind) are all nouns denoting locality. They can be used alone or together with such words as 边 or 面.

1. 房间里有三个人。
2. 安娜坐在我的右边。
3. 真糟糕,前边堵车了!
4. 请你们到外面去说话,我要睡觉了。

二、"离",介词,由"离"组成的介词结构在句子中作状语,表示时间和空间的距离。例如:

离 is a preposition. The prepositional phrase formed by 离 functions as adverbial in a sentence, indicating the temporal or spatial distance.

1. 我的家离公司很近,可以走着去上班。
2. 我们学校离长城饭店远吗?
3. 今天,离考试还有一个星期。
4. 离上次拜访没有几天,你就不认识我了?

三、"可",副词,与"不"构成反问句式"可不"、"可不是",形式上是否定的,却是用较强烈的语气表示肯定、赞同。例如:

可 is an adverb, which can be used together with 不 to form rhetorical questions introduced by 可不 or 可不是. Such sentences are negative in form, but express affirmation or agreement in a rather strong tone.

A:你最好去公司工作。
B:可不,我也这么想!

A:现在正是上下班时间,走哪儿都堵车。
B:可不是,你说得一点儿都不错。

补充生词
Additional New Words

左　　zuǒ　　　left
右　　yòu　　　right
外　　wài　　　outside, outward

练习
Exercises

一、**替换练习**:

Substitution drills:

A:你住在哪儿?
B:我住在<u>学校的四号楼</u>。
A:<u>杰克</u>也住<u>四号楼</u>吗?
B:不,<u>杰克</u>住<u>三号楼</u>。

留学生楼	安娜	学校的一号楼
芳庄公寓	山口	亚运村公寓
友谊宾馆	史特凡	长城饭店
中国朋友家	谢文	他的爸爸妈妈家

A:你住的学生宿舍一个月付多少房租?
B:一个月70美元。
A:谁付?
B:我自己。

留学生楼	240	我爸
公寓	450	学校
饭店	3200	公司
宾馆	4600	老板

二、把下面的词组成句子:

Unscramble the following into normal sentences:

1. 我 在 四号 房间 住 215 楼

2. 我 没有 房间 电话 的 里

3. 打 很 方便 我们 不 电话

4. 不 住 外边 学校 喜欢 我们 在

5. 名片 电话 地址 我 和 的 上 有

6. 星期天 我们 老师 去 拜访

7. 学校 错 我们 环境 不 的

三、完成对话:

Complete the following dialogues:

A:你觉得留学生公寓的房租贵吗?
B:_____。

A：_____？
B：我喜欢住在中国朋友家。

A：你为什么不住在学校里边？
B：_____。

A：你认为住在学校里边方便还是住学校外边方便？
B：_____。

A：你住的公寓环境怎么样？
B：_____。

四、熟读下面的词语，然后用其中的五个词造句：

Read and memorize the following words, and then choose five of them to make sentences with：

里边	外边	上边	下边
左边	右边	前边	后边
里面	外面	上面	下面
左面	右面	前面	后面
以前	以后	以上	以下

五、选择练习四里合适的词语填空：

Fill in the blanks with appropriate nouns occuring in exercise 4：

1. 我们学校的环境很好，____是商店，____是饭店，很方便。
2. 对不起，房间____有人睡觉，不能进去。
3. 太太和先生很有意思，在家____先生听太太的，在家____

太太听先生的。
4. 开车____要系好安全带。
5. 我们都住在留学生公寓,男学生住在____女学生住在____。
6. 黑板____写着今天学习的生词。
7. 经理特别客气,把我们送到____才回去。
8. 老板的事太多,吃饭____就开始工作。

六、用"可不"、"可不是"完成对话:

Complete the following dialogues with 可不 or 可不是:

A:发高烧得去医院检查。
B:____,____。
A:住得离学校太远,可不方便。
B:____,____。
A:学习汉语有问题应该问老师。
B:____,____。
A:你住在长城饭店,房租很贵吧?
B:____,____。

七、会话练习:

Situational conversations:

情景1:你入学时,向留学生部申请住房。
　　Apply to the Department of Foreign Students for accommodation.
情景2:你在校外向房屋出租者租房。
　　Rent a room from outside the university.

八、读拼音，写汉字：

Read the following passage and then write it out in Chinese characters:

Rìběn liúxuéshēng Shānkǒu, bù zhù xuéxiào, zhù zài Yàyùncūn. Yàyùncūn lí xuéxiào bù yuǎn, huánjìng hěn hǎo, gòuwù, yúlè, dōu hěn fāngbiàn. Gōngyù lǐ hái yǒu diànhuà. Dāngrán, Shānkǒu zuì gāoxìng de shì, tā bùyòng fù fángzū. Tā qǐng lǎoshī hé tóngxuémen qù tā jiā wánr. Tóngxuémen shuō, tāmen yǒukòng jiù qù bàifǎng Shānkǒu.

第二十二课　住在哪儿（二）
Lesson 22 Where Are You Staying（2）

课文
Text

在课外

珍　妮：嗨,山口,在这儿遇上你了!
山　口：真的,怎么这么巧!
杰　克：山口,你来买什么?
山　口：我来买些家用电器。
珍　妮：亚运村公寓没有电视、冰箱、洗衣机吗?
山　口：有。我想有一个家庭电影院。
珍　妮：啊,这可要花一大笔钱!
山　口：是啊,你们能去帮我好好挑挑吗?
珍　妮：好,我们一起去!

售货员：小姐,欢迎惠顾本店!
山　口：你能给我们介绍介绍商品吗?
售货员：小姐想买什么?

山　口：我要买几件家用电器。
售货员：好的,请跟我来。
山　口：你们管送吗？
售货员：管。我们免费送货上门。
杰　克：什么门？楼门还是家门？
珍　妮：我听说,送货上门,就是送到大楼的楼门口。
山　口：我可住在22层！
售货员：请放心,我们保证送到22层你的家里。
山　口：我买好你们就给送吗？
售货员：小姐住哪儿？
山　口：我家在亚运村。
售货员：亚运村离我们商场太远了,恐怕一个星期才能送到。
山　口：这么长的时间？不能马上送吗？
售货员：不能。商店又不是为你一个人服务,我们忙不过来！
杰　克：山口,我们走,找一家离亚运村近一点儿的商店。
珍　妮：走！商店不想赚这个钱,我们还不想买了呢！
售货员：啊,小姐,你买吧,我们立即送货上门！

生词

New Words

1.	遇上	yùshàng	meet
2.	巧	qiǎo	coincidental, skilful, artful
3.	些	xiē	some, a few, a little

4.	电器	diànqì	electrical appliances
5.	电视	diànshì	television
6.	冰箱	bīngxiāng	refrigerator
7.	洗衣机	xǐyījī	washing machine
8.	家庭	jiātíng	family, household
9.	电影院	diànyǐngyuàn	cinema
10.	惠顾	huìgù	your patronage
11.	本店	běndiàn	this store
12.	商品	shāngpǐn	commodity, goods
13.	跟	gēn	follow; with
14.	件	jiàn	single item
15.	管	guǎn	provide, guarantee, manage
16.	免费	miǎnfèi	free of charge
17.	放心	fàngxīn	be at ease, rest assured
18.	保证	bǎozhèng	pledge, guarantee
19.	长	cháng	long; length, strong point
20.	恐怕	kǒngpà	fear, be afraid of; perhaps
21.	服务	fúwù	serve; service
22.	忙	máng	busy
23.	马上	mǎshàng	immediately, at once
24.	立即	lìjí	at once, promptly

注释
Notes

一、"些",不定量词,它前面的数词只能用"一",不能用其它数词。

例如：

些（some, a few, a little）is an indefinite measure word, which can be preceded only by the numeral 一（one）and not any other numerals.

　　一些书　　　一些笔　　　一些香蕉
　　一些同学　　一些朋友　　一些老大妈

"些"还常常用在代词"这、那、哪"的后边。例如：
些 is also often used after such pronouns as 这（this），那（that）and 哪（which）.

　　这些钱　　　这些花　　　这些客人
　　那些货　　　那些车　　　那些司机
　　哪些房间　　哪些优点　　哪些问题

二、"恐怕",副词,表示估计,大体上肯定某事即将发生,但又不是很有把握;有时还表示出某种担心。"恐怕"的后边,常常有助动词"要、能、得"等相呼应。例如：

恐怕, as an adverb, indicates an estimate, more or less affirming that something will happen, but not being hundred percent certain. It sometimes expresses a certain degree of anxiety. 恐怕 often corresponds with such auxiliary verbs as 要, 能, and 得 that come afterwards.

1. 明天我恐怕不能来,你不要等我。
2. 这事儿,你恐怕得找经理。
3. 他恐怕已经走了二十多天了。
4. 你要是再误事,恐怕老板要开除你了！

"恐怕"有时候还表达一种委婉的口气。说话人其实已经有了自己的想法,但用估计、商量的语气说出来。句尾常常有"吧"字。例如：

恐怕 sometimes expresses a mild tone. The speaker has actually formed his opinion, but expresses it in a tone of estimation or consultation. Such sentences often end with the character 吧.

1. 这恐怕不能吧。
2. 你这样做,恐怕不好吧!
3. 这个价格恐怕太高了吧!
4. 他们俩在这儿见面,恐怕不是巧遇吧!

三、"马上",副词,表示事情很快就要发生。例如：

马上, adverb, indicates that something will happen very soon.

1. 出租车马上就来。
2. 你应该马上付房租。
3. 我马上就去见经理。
4. 你马上打电话叫她来!

"马上"还表示两件事接连发生,后一件事情紧接着前一件事情。例如：

马上 also indicates that two things happen consecutively, with the second happening right after the first.

你先去吧,我马上就来。

我下班后马上回家。

他听了我的话,好像马上想起了什么。

他刚走,看样子不会马上回来。

"立即",也是副词,意思和用法与"马上"基本相同,上面各句中的"马上"都可以换成"立即"。只是"马上"多用于口语,而"立即"更常用于书面。

立即 is also an adverb, whose meaning and usage are basically the same as 马上. 马上 in the previous examples can all be replaced by 立即. The only difference is that 马上 is more often used in spoken Chinese, while 立即 is used more often in written Chinese.

练习
Exercises

一、**替换练习**:

Substitution drills:

A:你们管<u>吃</u>吗?

B:我们管,<u>一日三餐都免费</u>。

送货上门	免费送货
退货	不问为什么
介绍商品	好就说好,不好就说不好
售后服务	免费上门服务

A:你保证今天送货吗？
B:我恐怕不能。
A:为什么？
B:我忙不过来。

不迟到	常常忘了时间
这些电器没问题	也不识货
这是巧遇	知道你会在这儿
给我打电话	有太多的约会

二、把下面的词组成句子：
Unscramble the following into normal sentences：

1. 我 遇到 王府井 老朋友 在 一个 今天

2. 这 巧 真是 太 了

3. 我们 洗衣机 用 衣服 洗

4. 现在 都 一些 电器 家家 有 家用

5. 他们 上门 保证 服务 免费

三、完成对话：
Complete the following dialogues：

A:贵国的商店管送货上门吗？
B:_____。

A:你们送的货会有问题吗？

B：你放心，_____。

A：_____？
B：我常常请售货员帮我挑选商品。

A：你们为什么不能马上送来？
B：_____。

四、从下面选择适当的量词填空：

Fill in the blanks with appropriate measure words：

件　些　笔　辆　瓶　次　点儿

1. 我要赚____钱去旅行。
2. 这____生意，他赚了不少钱。
3. 你这是第几____迟到了？
4. 出门不带____现金不方便。
5. 我买了一____新车。
6. 她只吃了一____东西就睡了。
7. 巧了，这____人我都认识。
8. 做什么事都只能一____一____地做。
9. 这____问题，我不能立即回答。
10. 他去看朋友的时候，带了一____葡萄酒。

五、用"恐怕"和括号里的词完成下面的句子：

Complete the following sentences with 恐怕 and the words in brackets：

1. 这么晚了，_____。（出租车）

215

2. 他病得很厉害,____。(住医院)
3. 我几天都没接到她的电话了,____。(不在北京)
4. 现在常常堵车,____。(早一点儿)
5. 你要是再误事,____。(开除)
6. 我现在很忙,____。(马上)

六、会话练习:

Situational conversations:

情景1:在商店买东西,同商家谈送货上门的事。
　　You are shopping at a store. Discuss with the assistant about delivery to domicile.
情景2:打电话给商家,要求上门服务。
　　Phone a shop to ask for service at home.

七、读拼音,写汉字:

Read the following passage and then write it out in Chinese characters:

　　Shānkǒu qù yī jiā shāngdiàn mǎi dōngxi, qiǎo yù Jiékè hé Zhēnní. Shānkǒu qǐng tāmen bāng tā tiāoxuǎn shāngpǐn. Jiékè hé Zhēnní zhēn xíng. Shāngdiàn shuō, yào yī gè xīngqī cáinéng bǎ huò sòngdào Shānkǒu jiā, Jiékè hé Zhēnní jiù xiàng kǎn jià yīyàng, sān shuō liǎng shuō, jiù ràng shāngdiàn lìjí sòng huò shàng mén.

第二十三课　今天怎么样（一）
Lesson 23　What's the Weather Like Today（1）

课文
Text

在课内

杰　克：安娜，今天怎么样？
安　娜：今天我的身体很好！
杰　克：我知道你的病早就好了，身体很好。
安　娜：那你问什么？
杰　克：我问今天天气怎么样？
安　娜：嗯……看样子不错。
杰　克：最高气温多少度？
安　娜：我不知道。
杰　克：你没听天气预报？
安　娜：我哪里听得懂！
杰　克：我们去问问老师吧！

安　娜:王老师,我们怎么听天气预报?
王老师:啊,这很容易。我这儿正好有今天的天气预报录音,你们听听。
安　娜:那太好了!

听众朋友们,你们好!现在播送 24 小时城市天气预报:北京,今天晚上多云转阴,有小雨雪,最低气温零下 7℃;明天白天,多云转晴,风力二、三级,最高气温 2℃。

王老师:你们听懂了吗?
杰　克:听懂了一点儿。
安　娜:我一点儿也没有听懂。
王老师:别着急,多听几遍就会听懂的。

生词
New Words

1.	身体	shēntǐ	body, health
2.	天气	tiānqì	weather
3.	看样子	kànyàngzi	look like, look as if
4.	气温	qìwēn	air temperature
5.	预报	yùbào	forecast
6.	哪里	nǎli	(used in rhetorical questions to express negation); where
7.	懂	dǒng	understand, know

8.	正好	zhènghǎo	just in time, just right, happen to
9.	录音	lùyīn	recording
10.	听众	tīngzhòng	audience, listeners
11.	播送	bōsòng	broadcast, transmit
12.	城市	chéngshì	city
13.	雨	yǔ	rain
14.	雪	xuě	snow
15.	零下	língxià	below zero
16.	白天	báitiān	daytime, day
17.	阴	yīn	overcast, shade
18.	云	yún	cloud
19.	晴	qíng	clear, fine
20.	风力	fēnglì	wind-force, wind power
21.	着急	zháojí	worried, anxious
22.	遍	biàn	once through; a time; all over

注释
Notes

一、"看样子",意思是看情形,看趋势。表示一种估计。例如:
看样子 has the meaning of judging by the circumstances or tendency. It expresses a kind of estimate.

1. 看样子他今天不会来了。
2. 看样子今天要下雨。
3. 看样子,这事不那么容易做好。

4. 风停了,看样子今天是个晴天。

二、"哪里",代词,表处所,如"你从哪里来?";也可以用在反问句中表示否定,这时没有处所的意思;用来单独答话,表示否定,是一种客气的说法。例如:

哪里, pronoun, indicates a place, as in "Where are you from?"(你从哪里来?) It can also be used in a rhetorical question to mean negation. In this case it doesn't indicate a place. When it is used as a reply by itself, it shows negation and is a polite way of expression.

1. 你从哪里来,我早听说了。
2. 他哪里是美国人,他是法国人。
3. 他哪里病了,他是不想上课。
4. 我哪里是什么大经理。
5. A:小姐,这事太麻烦你了!
   B:哪里,哪里,快别客气。

三、"正好",副词,表示两件事或两种情况的巧合。例如:

正好 is an adverb which indicates that two things or two circumstances just coincide with each other.

1. 现在天气很好,正好去旅行。
2. 这些钱正好买一张飞机票。
3. 这几天我正好休息,可以陪你去玩。
4. 她开始工作的时候,正好二十岁。

"正好",有时可以作句子的谓语、补语,有时还可以单独成句。这时的"正好"是个实词,意思相当于"正合适"。例如:

正好 can sometimes function as the predicate or complement of a sentence. Sometimes it can be used on its own. In that case, 正好 is a notional word, with its meaning being 正合适 (just right).

1. 你来得正好,经理刚从外边回来。
2. 这间办公室不大不小,正好。

A:多少钱?
B:十二元五角。
A:给你。
B:你的钱正好。

练习
Exercises

一、**替换练习**:
Substitution drills:

A:你爸爸的病怎么样?
B:看样子,他的病快好了。

身体	还不错
工作	很难找
生意	不大好做
旅行	很顺利

A:他没有听老师讲课?
B:他哪里听得懂。

去打工	有时间
去做生意	会做
买一辆车	有那么多钱
叫你一声	记得我这个老同学

A：你能陪我去<u>商店</u>吗？
B：行，我正好<u>休息</u>。

书店	想买几本书
医院	要去拿点儿药
留学生办公室	要去交学费
听力室	想听天气预报录音

二、把下面的词组成句子：

Unscramble the following into normal sentences：

1. 你　怎么样　身体　的

2. 今天　多少　气温　最高　白天　度

3. 我　大　预报　不　天气　相信

4. 他　工作　着急　找　不

5. 请　说　一遍　你　再

三、完成对话：

Complete the following dialogues：

A：你常常听天气预报吗？
B：不，_____。

A：你旅行的时候，喜欢什么样的天气？
B：_____。

A：你旅行的时候，最怕遇上什么样的天气？

B：_____。

A：下雨天，你在家都做些什么？
B：_____。

A：_____？
B：别着急，你只是感冒了，不是什么大病。

四、模仿例句说话：

Make sentences according to the example：

例句：看样子，今天天气不错。

1. 他俩的友谊

2. 这辆汽车

3. 出租车

4. 着急

5. 容易做

五、下面是天气预报的常用词，先熟读，然后听一听、说一说今天的天气预报：

Read and familiarize yourself with the following words which are often used in weather forecast. Then listen to and talk about the weather forecast of today：

白天—晚上(夜间)　　最高—最低　　阴—晴

223

气温　度　零下　云　雨　雪　风
风力　级　转

六、会话练习：
Situational conversation：

情景：朋友见面,开始总是先问好,然后谈今天天气怎么样。听,两个朋友的谈话就这样开始了。……
When friends meet, they first greet each other and then start talking about the weather. Here are two friends talking in this way.

七、读拼音,写汉字：
Read the following passage and then write it out in Chinese characters：

Jīntiān de kǒuyǔ kè, tóngxuémen xuéxí zěnme tīng tiānqì yùbào. Tiānqì yùbào shuō, wǎnshang yǒu yǔ, zuì dī wēndù língxià qī dù. Míngtiān báitiān duō yún zhuǎn qíng, fēnglì bù dà, zuì gāo wēndù shí'èr dù. Míngtiān tiānqì bù cuò, Jiékè, Zhēnní hé Shānkǒu zhǔnbèi jìnchéng.

第二十四课　今天怎么样(二)
Lesson 24　What's the Weather Like Today (2)

课文
Text

在课外

珍　妮：杰克，你看，好像要下雨了！
杰　克：你不是说，天气预报今天没有雨吗？
山　口：珍妮还说今天天气好呢！
珍　妮：天气预报是这么说的嘛！怎么说变天就变天了呢？
杰　克：老师说过，北京天气的特点，是夏天多雨，冬天多雪，春天多风。
山　口：北京的秋天最好，没风少雨，不冷不热。
珍　妮：我忘了老师的话了，现在正是多雨的季节，出门的时候就应该带上雨衣。
山　口：我们骑着自行车，现在怎么回学校呢？
杰　克：我有办法，跟我来！

杰　克：小姐，我们遇上雨了，没有带雨具，可以借给我们吗？
小　姐：当然可以。要雨衣还是雨伞？
杰　克：我们骑自行车，要雨衣。
小　姐：好的。
杰　克：我们必须什么时候还回来？
小　姐：你们来商店的时候，顺便带来就可以了。
杰　克：必须送到你们商店来吗？
小　姐：啊，不。本市几十家商场都有这项服务，你们可以送到离你们最近的一家商店。
杰　克：谢谢！

珍　妮：杰克，你好像跟那位小姐很熟？
杰　克：不。我们不认识。
珍　妮：那你怎么知道她肯借给你雨具？
杰　克：中国朋友告诉我，在商店可以借到雨具。
山　口：商店不怕借的人不还吗？
杰　克：文明伞，大家用。相信大家都讲文明嘛！

生词
New Words

1. 变　　　biàn　　　　change, transform
2. 特点　　tèdiǎn　　　characteristic
3. 夏天　　xiàtiān　　　summer
4. 冬天　　dōngtiān　　winter

5.	秋天	qiūtiān	autumn
6.	冷	lěng	cold
7.	热	rè	hot
8.	季节	jìjié	season
9.	出门	chūmén	go out, leave home, go on a journey
10.	雨衣	yǔyī	raincoat
11.	骑	qí	ride, sit on the back of
12.	自行车	zìxíngchē	bicycle
13.	办法	bànfǎ	way, means, measure
14.	雨具	yǔjù	rain gear
15.	借	jiè	borrow, lend
16.	雨伞	yǔsǎn	umbrella
17.	必须	bìxū	must, have to
18.	商场	shāngchǎng	market, bazaar, department store
19.	还	huán	give back, return, go back
20.	顺便	shùnbiàn	without much extra effort
21.	位	wèi	(measure word for people)
22.	熟	shú	familiar, well-acquainted, ripe, cooked
23.	肯	kěn	be willing to, agree, consent
24.	本市	běnshì	this city
25.	项	xiàng	(measure word for itemized things)
26.	文明	wénmíng	civilization; civilized

注释
Notes

一、趋向补语：一些动词后边常用"来、去、上、下、上来、下去、起来、出去、进来"等词作补语，表示动作的方向。例如：

Directional complement: Some verbs take such words as 来 (come), 去(go), 上(up), 下(down), 上来(come up), 下去(go down), 起来(arise), 出去(go out), 进来(come in), etc. as the complement, indicating the direction of movement.

1. 谁呀？请进来！
2. 我看见汽车已经开出去了。
3. 请你站起来说吧！
4. 这天真的下起雨来了。

二、"跟"，介词，介绍出动作的另一个施动者。当一个动作有两个参与者时，"跟"字前面的施动者处于主导地位，两个施动者的前后顺序不能颠倒。例如：

跟 is a preposition to introduce the other agent of an action. When an action has two participants, the one mentioned before 跟 is in the dominant position, and they cannot be transposed.

1. 我跟她吵？是她跟我吵！
2. 我不跟他说话，我们没有什么好说的。
3. 不是我不想跟她好，是她不想跟我好。

介绍出动作的对象。例如：
跟 can also introduce the recipient of an action.

1. 你快跟大家说说,她的病怎么样了。
2. 你别走,我跟你说点儿事。
3. 我现在没有钱,我可以跟朋友借。

补充生词
Additional New Words

吵(架)	chǎo(jià)	quarrel, have a row
干燥	gānzào	dry, arid
潮湿	cháoshī	moist, damp
凉快	liángkuai	cool, nice and cool
暖和	nuǎnhuo	warm, nice and warm

练习
Exercises

一、替换练习:
Substitution drills:

A:我们必须什么时候来?
B:你们最好在八点以前来。

出差	下星期三
离开宾馆	十二点
去机场	飞机起飞
安排好饭	老板来检查

A:你好像跟那位小姐 认识?
B:我们见过两次面。

万文杰	很熟悉	我们是朋友
什么人	吵架了	有的人真没礼貌
公司	有点儿麻烦	麻烦还不小
老板	说了些什么	我想让他明白一些事

二、把下面的词组成句子：

Unscramble the following into normal sentences：

1. 她 电话 的 变 号码 了

2. 北京 干燥 冬天 春天 的 很 和

3. 很 喜欢 多 骑 人 自行车

4. 你 办法 什么 好 有 吗

5. 你 大家 肯 都 帮助

三、完成对话：

Complete the following dialogues：

A：北京什么季节多风？
B：_____。

A：你喜欢骑自行车旅行吗？
B：_____。

A：_____？

B:我们去买一把雨伞吧!

A:你不怕我借了你的钱不还吗?
B:＿＿＿＿＿＿＿＿。

A:你去请他,他肯来吗?
B:不,＿＿＿＿＿＿＿＿。

四、模仿例句说话:

Make sentences according to the example:

例句:刚才还是好天气,怎么说变就变了呢?

1. 吵架

2. 不来

3. 开除

4. 取消

5. 收费

五、选词填空:

Fill in the blanks with the words provided:

顺便　　随便　　方便

1. 你们想喝什么就喝什么,请别客气,我的家很＿＿＿＿＿。

231

2. 你去银行能_____为我兑换点钱吗？
3. 这儿环境很好。买东西,娱乐,都很_____。
4. 你别看他很有钱,吃东西不讲究,很_____。
5. 我们这儿,上班喝咖啡免费,很_____。
6. 出门旅行带很多现金不_____。
7. 我来北京出差,_____拜访了多年没见的一位老朋友。
8. 请别误会,我只是_____问问。

特别　　特点

1. 这个酒吧很有_____,葡萄酒_____好。
2. 北京冬天_____干燥。
3. 不能随便交朋友,_____是女孩子。
4. 北京人说话很有_____,你说是吗？
5. 她的_____是跟什么人都见面熟。
6. 他有很多中国朋友,所以,他的听和说都_____好。
7. 快餐的_____就是快!
8. 你都说了,我没什么_____要说的。

六、填空:

Complete the following:

　　一年有___个季节。它们是___、___、___、___。北京的春天从___月到___月,夏天从___月到___月,秋天从___月到___月,冬天从___月到___月。北京的冬天最___,最___,很少下___。春天很___,不过常常___。夏天多___,白天有点儿___,不过晚上很___,会觉得很舒服。秋天最好,多___天,很少刮___下___,我不___北京的天气,现在慢慢___了。

七、会话练习：

Situational conversations：

1. 介绍贵国或你家乡的天气。
   Talk about the weather at home.
2. 杰克他们去的商店出借的雨伞为什么叫"文明伞"？商店为什么开展出借"文明伞"的服务？
   Talk about the umbrellas lent out by the store Jack and Jenny went to. Why do they provide this kind of service?

八、读拼音，写汉字：

Read the following passage, and then write it out in Chinese characters：

　　Jiékè, Zhēnní hé Shānkǒu yīqǐ jìnchéng, hǎohāor de qíngtiān shuō biàn jiù biàn, qíng zhuǎn yīn, yīhuìr, xià qǐ yǔ lái le. Tāmen dōu qí zìxíngchē, yòu méi dài yǔjù, zěnme bàn? Háishì Jiékè yǒu bànfǎ. Tā dài dàjiā dào yī jiā shāngdiàn, jiè le sān jiàn yǔyī. Zhēnní hé Shānkǒu dōu hěn qíguài, Jiékè zěnme néng zài shāngdiàn jiè dào yǔyī ne? Yuánlái shāngdiàn gěi gùkè zhǔnbèi le shuí dōu kěyǐ jiè de wénmíng sǎn.

第二十五课　逛北京(一)
Lesson 25 Roaming Around Beijing(1)

课文
Text

在课内

王老师:同学们,你们来北京多久了?
杰　克:我来北京快一年了。
珍　妮:我来了还不到半年。
王老师:你们逛过北京了吗?
杰　克:我和珍妮常去。
王老师:山口呢?
山　口:我坐出租车进过几次城。
杰　克:那还叫逛?骑自行车去才叫逛呢!
山　口:我不认路,骑自行车出去,怕回不了家。
珍　妮:找个人带路啊!
山　口:找谁?
杰　克:我啊!我是个老北京了。

王老师：杰克，你说你是老北京？
杰　克：不好意思，开开玩笑。
王老师：你到底熟悉不熟悉北京呢？
杰　克：说不上熟悉，不过骑自行车进城，丢不了。
山　口：你有什么办法？
杰　克：这很简单。北京的大街、胡同、马路，都是笔直笔直的，不是南北方向，就是东西方向。
珍　妮：只要记住我们学校在什么地方，就丢不了。
山　口：那也不行，我分不清东西南北。
杰　克：这也有办法，你只要记住向左拐，往右拐……
山　口：不行，不行。拐来拐去，还不拐糊涂了！
珍　妮：山口，你还是花钱坐出租车吧。坐出租车不会糊涂，哈，哈，哈……

生词
New Words

1. 久　　jiǔ　　　　long; for a long time
2. 逛　　guàng　　　stroll, ramble, roam
3. 带路　dàilù　　　lead the way, act as a guide
4. 玩笑　wánxiào　　joke, jest
5. 到底　dàodǐ　　　finally, on earth, after all
6. 丢　　diū　　　　lose, mislay, put aside
7. 大街　dàjiē　　　main street
8. 胡同　hútòngr　　lane, alley
9. 马路　mǎlù　　　road, street, avenue

235

10.	笔直	bǐzhí	perfectly straight
11.	东	dōng	east
12.	南	nán	south
13.	西	xī	west
14.	北	běi	north
15.	方向	fāngxiàng	direction, orientation
16.	分	fēn	divide, distinguish
17.	清楚	qīngchu	clear, distinct
18.	向	xiàng	direction; turn towards
19.	往	wǎng	go; in the direction of, towards
20.	拐	guǎi	turn
21.	糊涂	hútu	muddled, confused
22.	地方	dìfang	place, locality

专名
Proper Nouns

北海公园	Běihǎi gōngyuán	Beihai Park
颐和园	Yíhéyuán	Summer Palace
天安门	Tiān'ānmén	Tian'anmen

注释
Notes

一、"到底",副词,用在疑问句中,追究事情的真相。句中或句尾常

有疑问词,或全句是一个选择式问句。例如:

到底 is an adverb to be used in an interrogative sentence to look into the actual state of affairs. Such a sentence normally contains an interrogative word in the middle or at the end of it, or the whole sentence is an alternative question.

1. 你快说,到底怎么了?
2. 你们说啊,到底是谁把雨伞拿走了?
3. 这件事,他到底清楚不清楚啊?
4. 你到底是去还是不去?大家都在等你呢!

二、"往",介词,与表方位或地点的词语组成介词词组,表示行为或动作的方向,可在句子中作状语。例如:

往 is a preposition used to form a prepositional phrase with words denoting direction or location. The prepositional phrase thus formed indicates the direction of an action or movement, functioning as an adverbial in the sentence.

1. 你往前走,就能看见我们学校了。
2. 往南走不远就是 368 路车站。
3. 你往后看,谁来了?
4. 师傅,请再往前开一点儿!

"往"组成的介词词组,也可以作补语或定语,这时"往"要读轻声,跟在它后边的多是表地点的词语,而不是方位词。例如:

Prepositional phrase with 往 can also function as a complement or an attribute. Under such circumstances, 往 should be read in the light tone, and the words that follow it are often words denoting places rather than directions.

1. 请问,这是开往上海的火车吗?
2. 这些是送往长城饭店的鲜花。
3. 飞往纽约(Niǔyuē new york)的班机已经起飞了。

三、"向",介词。由"向"组成的介词词组,表示动作的方向或趋向。这时同"往"的意义和用法差不多。例如:

向 is a preposition used to form a prepositional phrase denoting the orientation or direction. In such cases,向 is similar to 往 in meaning and usage.

1. 师傅,请向右拐。
2. 他向胡同口走去。
3. 向前走三个房间,就是王老师的办公室。
4. 我们一起走向美好的明天!

"向"还可以介绍出行为和动作的对象。例如:

向 is also used to introduce the object of an action or behavior.

1. 我向大家介绍一下,这是我们公司的总裁万先生。
2. 这事儿,你向她说清楚了吗?
3. 我要向他学习。
4. 你如果遇到什么麻烦,就向大家说吧,大家会帮助你的。

四、"不是……就是……",这种"不是 A 就是 B"的格式中,前后两项中必有一项是事实。例如:

不是…就是…: In this pattern of "If not A, then it must be B", A and B should be verbs or adjectives of the same type.

They can also be clauses. One of the two must be factual.

1. 不是你去,就是我去。
2. 这天,不是刮风就是下雨。
3. 今天吃饭,不是你付钱就是我付钱。

五、"胡同",就是城市里比较狭窄的小街道,一般称作"巷",与宽阔的大街相对而言,所谓"大街小巷"。只是以北京为中心的几个北方城市叫小巷为"胡同",中国的其它城市不这么叫。尤其是在北京,"胡同"好像是北京城市的独特景观。人们说起胡同,就自然会想到北京;说起北京,就自然会想到它的胡同。北京的胡同旅游,是近几年来北京最吸引外国人的特色旅游。

胡同 is a narrow lane in a city. It is normally referred to as 巷, contrasting with wide streets, as in 大街小巷 (wide streets and small lanes). It is only in a few northern cities around Beijing that lanes are referred to as 胡同, and not in other cities. 胡同 seems to be a unique scenery in the city of Beijing. Whenever 胡同 is mentioned, people will think of Beijing; and whenever Beijing is mentioned, people will think of its 胡同. Touring Beijing's 胡同 is a distinctive touring item in Beijing that is developed in recent years and is most attractive to foreign friends.

练习
Exercises

一、**替换练习**:

Substitution drills:

A:你来北京多久了？
B:我来北京<u>三个月</u>了。
A:你去过<u>天安门</u>吗？
B:我去过一次。

半年	王府井
一年	长城
一个学期	颐和园
一年零两个月	上海

A:你去哪儿？
B:<u>逛商店</u>。
A:你一个人去的吗？
B:不,我跟<u>山口</u>一起去的。

西单	安娜
王府井	杰克
北海公园	珍妮
颐和园	一个中国朋友

A:你到底<u>认识</u>不<u>认识</u><u>钱先生</u>？
B:<u>认识</u>,不过不<u>熟悉</u>。

喜欢	这种手表	想买
了解	马小姐	来往
知道	这件事	清楚
听	老板的话	照他说的做

二、把下面的词组成句子：

Unscramble the following into normal sentences：

1. 这　个　玩笑　是　只　开

2. 我　喜欢　这　玩笑　不　个

3. 你　什么　了　丢

4. 我　自行车　了　丢　的

5. 今天　真　糊涂　我

6. 你们　在　地方　学校　什么

7. 这　问题　很　个　简单

三、完成对话：

Complete the following dialogues：

A：你能分清东西南北吗？
B：不，_____。

A：你们公司在什么地方？
B：_____。

A：_____？
B：你跟我来，我带你去。

A：你知道他为什么没来上班吗？
B：不很清楚,他好像_____。

四、模仿例句说话：

Make sentences according to the example：

例句：北京的大街,不是南北方向,就是东西方向。

1. 星期天　　宿舍　　教室

2. 太太出门　　开车　　叫出租车

3. 我的手表坏了　　快　　慢

4. 杰克进城　　走路　　骑自行车

5. 他有点儿糊涂　　拿错书　　忘了上课时间

五、为下列各句填上合适的介词：

Fill in the blanks with the prepositions given：

从　往　向

1. 不能上课要____老师请假。
2. 你____哪儿走？已经到了。
3. 上班时，经理总是先____大家问好。
4. ____前走，就对了；____后退，就错了。
5. 不要觉得总是自己对，要多听听别人怎么说，要____别人学习。
6. 他记得____去年夏天开始，他不怕说汉语了。
7. ____北京人问路，他告诉你____南拐，____前走到十字路口，再____北拐就到了；____上海人问路，他告诉你____左拐，____前走到十字路口，再____右拐就到了，很有意思。
8. 我们三个人都是____南方来的。

六、下面是北京市示意图，请你按下面的要求说说骑自行车怎样去目的地：

Below is a sketch map of Beijing. Please explain how you can get to the required destinations by bike.

说话时用上下面的词：

You have to use the following words in your talk：

向　往　拐　一直　左　右　前　后　东　西

南　北　从　到

例如：从经贸大学骑自行车去天安门，怎么走？

模仿这个例子说话。

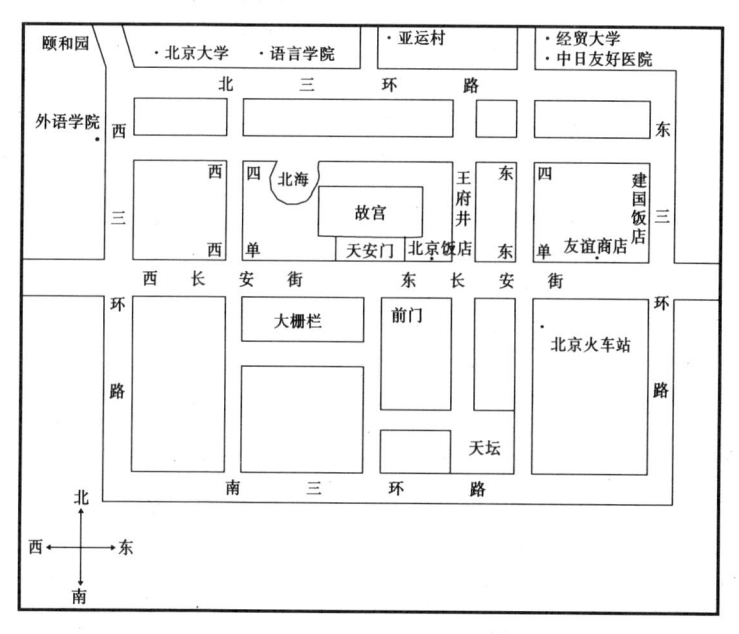

(地图：颐和园、北京大学、语言学院、亚运村、经贸大学、中日友好医院、外语学院、北三环路、西三环路、北海、故宫、王府井、建国饭店、四、西单、天安门、北京饭店、东单、友谊商店、西长安街、东长安街、东三环路、大栅栏、前门、北京火车站、天坛、南三环路)

北 西→东 南

七、朗读下面的拼音，试一试能不能用汉字把这段话写出来：

Read aloud the following, and try to put it into Chinese characters：

绕口令和对联 Tongue twisters and antithetical couplets：

Māma qí mǎ mǎ màn māma mà mǎ

(Mum is riding a horse. The horse is slow, and Mum scolds the horse.)

Shūshu zhòng shù shù shǎo shūshu shǔ shù

(Uncle is planting trees. Some trees are missing, and Uncle counts the trees.)

shí bú shì sì sì bú shì shí (Ten is not four; four is not ten.)
shí sì shì shí sì (Fourteen is fourteen;)
sì shí shì sì shí (and forty is forty;)
tiān èr jiù shì shí gè shí (Plus two you yet a hundred.)

第二十六课　逛北京(二)
Lesson 26 Roaming Around Beijing (2)

课文
Text

在课外

山　口:杰克,我们去哪儿?
杰　克:先去王府井,然后去前门大栅栏和西单。
山　口:为什么去那儿?
珍　妮:这是北京最繁华的三条商业街。
山　口:好,走吧,我跟着你们。
杰　克:前面就是王府井了,我们把车存在这儿吧,走的时候好取。
山　口:嚼,好热闹!门脸挨着门脸,商店真多啊!
珍　妮:听,那儿在吆喝什么?

"站一站,看一看,出口转内销啰!"

"迷你美容霜,女人化妆佳品,买一送一啰!"

杰　克:听不大懂,好像是叫人停下来买他的东西。
山　口:走,去看看!

杰　克:我们到西单北大街了!
山　口:这儿跟大栅栏不一样嘛,倒是跟王府井差不多。
珍　妮:大栅栏是条传统商业街,街道窄,门面古色古香。
杰　克:王府井和西单,是现代化商业街,高楼大厦,好气派!
珍　妮:在世界各地能买到的,在这些商店差不多都能买到。
山　口:真的?都是进口货吗?
杰　克:不!进口货,中国货,什么都有得卖,什么也都有人买。
珍　妮:中国真是人多,商店多,东西多,卖什么都有人买,生意好做,钱好赚。
山　口:听你这口气,你好像已经在中国市场上赚了大钱了!
杰　克:哈,恭喜发财!
珍　妮:同喜!同喜!

生词
New Words

1.	然后	ránhòu	then, afterwards
2.	繁华	fánhuá	flourishing, bustling, busy
3.	条	tiáo	(measure word for long or narrow or thin things)
4.	商业	shāngyè	commerce
5.	存	cún	leave with, check, deposit
6.	取	qǔ	take, get, fetch
7.	热闹	rènao	lively, bustling with noise and excitement
8.	门脸	ménliǎn	shop front
9.	挨	āi	be next to
10.	嗬	hē	ah, oh
11.	吆喝	yāohe	cry out, call, shout
12.	出口	chūkǒu	export, speak, exit
13.	内销	nèixiāo	domestic sale
14.	迷	mí	confuse, fascinate, be crazy about; fan
15.	美容霜	měiróngshuāng	beauty cream
16.	化妆	huàzhuāng	make up
17.	佳品	jiāpǐn	excellent product
18.	倒是	dàoshì	(indicating concession, contrast, or sth. unexpected)

19.	差不多	chàbuduō	about the same, similar, almost
20.	传统	chuántǒng	tradition
21.	门面	ménmiàn	the facade of a shop, appearance
22.	古色古香	gǔsègǔxiāng	antique, quaint
23.	现代化	xiàndàihuà	modernization; modernize; modern
24.	大厦	dàshà	large building, mansion
25.	气派	qìpài	imposing manner, dignified air
26.	世界	shìjiè	world
27.	各地	gèdì	various places
28.	进口	jìnkǒu	import; entrance
29.	口气	kǒuqì	tone, note, manner of speaking
30.	恭喜	gōngxǐ	congratulate
31.	发财	fācái	get rich, make a fortune

专名

Proper Nouns

前门	Qiánmén	Qianmen
大栅栏	Dàzhàlán	Dazhalan

注释
Notes

一、"跟",介词,引出表比较对象。"跟"后面常有"相同"、"一样"、"差不多"、"相反"等词语相呼应。例如:

跟 is a preposition introducing the object of comparison. 跟 often corresponds with such words as 相同 (identical), 一样(the same), 差不多(about the same), or 相反(the opposite).

1. 我跟他一样,也是美国人。
2. 我跟他不一样,见了人他不爱说话,我爱说话。
3. 这辆车跟那辆车的价钱差不多。
4. "门脸"跟"门面"的意思差不多。

二、"倒是",副词,表示不以为然,或强调与事实相反,或表示让步。例如:

倒是 is an adverb expressing disapproval, stressing that it is contrary to the fact, or expressing a concession.

1. 我倒是没什么,就怕她不高兴。
2. 他倒是说得容易,让他去试试看!
3. 东西倒是好,就是太贵了。
4. 我倒是想帮助你,只是手头没有钱。
5. 该说的你不说,不该说的你倒是说个没完。
6. 我的先生倒是天天回来,只是回来就要睡觉,难得同他说几句话。

"倒是"还可以表示催促、深究。例如:

倒是 is also used to express urging, or going into a matter seriously.

    1. 你倒是去还是不去？
    2. 你倒是快一点啊，汽车要开了！
    3. 你倒是去找她啊，有什么不好意思的！
    4. 到底怎么回事，你倒是说呀！

三、"恭喜发财"，这是中国很流行的一句客套话。在春节，人们见面，互相一拱手，就说"恭喜发财！"对对方表示新年的良好祝福。生意场上，人们见面，也常常用这句话表示问候和祝贺，甚至询问对方在哪儿做生意，也这样问："您在哪儿发财呀？"

恭喜发财 (Congratulations and may you be prosperous) is a polite formula which is very popular in China. During the Spring Festival, as soon as people meet, they would make a cupped-hand salute to each other and say: 恭喜发财, which is a New Year benediction on the other party. On the business arena, when people meet, they often use it as a greeting or benediction. Even when they ask the other party where they are doing business, they would say: Where are you making your fortune?

四、"差不多"，表示近似的意思，说明事件或情况跟某种程度、数量、性状等相差无几。有时是一种强调，有时是一种估计。例如：

差不多 means "similar", indicating that an event or a situation is not much different from a certain degree, quantity, or shape and properties. Sometimes it expresses an emphasis, and sometimes it is an estimate.

    1. 我的钱差不多都花完了。

2. 现在常常堵车,坐车跟走路差不多一样快。
3. 这三条街差不多一样繁华。
4. 他做生意差不多快三十年了。

"差一点"、"差点儿",是一个固定格式,跟"差不多"一样,也表示近似的意思,但用法不同。如果"差一点"后边所说的事情是说话人期望的,肯定形式表示否定的意思,否定形式表示肯定的意思。例如:

差一点 or 差点儿 is a set expression. Like 差不多, it also expresses similarity, but the usage is different. If what follows 差一点 is what the speaker expects, the positive form expresses a negative implication, and the negative form expresses a positive implication.

1. 这种化妆品,我差一点儿就买着了。(没买着)
2. 这种化妆品,我差一点儿没买着。(买着了)

3. 昨天我差一点找到了工作。(没找到)
4. 昨天我差一点没找到工作。(找到了)

"差一点"后边所说的事情如果是说话人不期望的,或无所谓是说话人期望、不期望的,那么不管肯定形式或否定形式,都是表示否定。例如:

If what follows 差一点 is not what the speaker expects, or if it is irrespective of his expectations, then both the positive and the negative forms express a negative implication.

1. 昨天我差点儿感冒了。(没感冒)
2. 昨天我差点儿没感冒。(没感冒)

3. 老板差点儿开除我。(没开除)
4. 老板差点儿没开除我。(没开除)

5. 上星期我差一点儿去了上海。(没去)
6. 上星期我差一点儿没去上海。(没去)

练习
Exercises

一、替换练习：

Substitution drills：

A：你觉得<u>他说的汉语</u>怎么样?
B：<u>他说的汉语</u>跟<u>你</u>差不多。

这家商店	别的商店
进口货	国产货
出口商品	内销商品
中国化妆品	外国化妆品

A：听你的口气，你好像考得很好!
B：你说得没错，<u>这次考试我得了 A</u>。

发财了	我刚赚了五万元
得了便宜	商家今天买一送一
找到了工作	我明天就上班
遇到了麻烦	我的自行车丢了

二、把下面的词组成句子：

Unscramble the following into normal sentences：

1. 我们 地方 存 找 个 车 吧

2. 要 存 收费 自行车 吗

3. 女人 都 很 出门 化妆 多

4. 很 进口 人 多 只 商品 相信

5. 你 应该 说话 用 不 口 这种

三、写出下列词语的反义词：

Give the antonym of the following：

大——　　　多——　　　买——
好——　　　进——　　　借——
对——　　　快——　　　远——
存——　　　冷——　　　贵——
难——　　　糊涂——　　潮湿——
进口——　　内销——　　优点——

四、完成对话：

Complete the following dialogues：

A：_____？
B：取车的时候交费。

A：那个人在吆喝什么？
B：_____。

253

A:你看这辆新车怎么样?
B:＿＿＿＿＿＿＿!

A:你倒是肯不肯借点钱给我?
B:＿＿＿＿＿＿＿。

A:恭喜发财!
B:＿＿＿,＿＿＿＿＿!

五、模仿例句说话:

Make sentences according to the example:

例句:这儿的环境倒是不错。

1. 很热闹

2. 一路顺利

3. 天气很好

4. 送人的佳品

5. 方向没错

例句:①这儿跟王府井差不多。
　　　②我差一点就记住了。
　　　③我差一点没记住。

1. 北京的房租

2. 遇到麻烦

3. 今天的外汇汇率

4. 发财

5. 北京好玩的地方

六、会话练习：

Situational conversations：

情景1：几个朋友骑自行车逛北京的商业街，边走，边看，边说。
Several friends are roaming around Beijing on bike. They look and talk on their way.

情景2：商店在吆喝"买一送一"，你相信这是好事，你的朋友不相信。你想出很多理由，想说服你的朋友。
Someone in a shop is shouting："Buy two for the price of one."You believe it is a good thing, while your friend doesn't. Try to persuade your friend.

七、朗读下面的拼音，试一试能不能用汉字把这段话写出来：

Read aloud the following, and try to put it into Chinese characters：

Nán Tōng zhōu Běi Tōng zhōu Nán běi Tōng zhōu tōng nán běi
(South Tongzhou, North Tongzhou, South and North Tongzhou link up the south and the north.)

Dōng biàn méi Xī biàn mén Dōng Xī biàn mén biàn dōng xī
(East side gate, west side gate, East and west side gates facilitate east-west communications.)

Chéng zhāo wǔ zhōu guì kè kè liú kè qù jiē wéi guì kè
(Sincerely we entertain distinguished guests from the five continents. Staying or leaving, they are all distinguished guests.)

Xiào yíng sì hǎi jiā bīn bīn lái bīn wǎng jìn shì jiā bīn
(Smilingly we welcome honoured guests from the four seas. Coming or going they are all honoured guests.)

Wèi jǐ máng wèi rén máng máng lǐ tōu xián hē hú xiāng chá xiāo xiāo hàn
(You are busy for yourself, and you are busy for the others. To snatch a little leisure from a busy life, please come and drink a pot of fragrant tea and dispel your sweat.)

Láo xīn kǔ láo lì kǔ kǔ zhōng qiú lè chī wǎn liángfěn qīng qīng xīn
(It's hard to work with one's brain, and it's hard to work with one's brawn. To find relief from your hardship, please come and have a bowl of bean jelly and clear up your mind.)

English Translation of the Texts

Lesson 1

HELLO

A: Hello.
B: Hello.

A: How do you do, Miss?
B: How do you do?

A: Hi, hello, Anna.
B: Hello, Jack.

A: Good morning, Anna.
B: Good morning, Jack.

A: Hi, Anna.
B: Hi, Jack.
A: How are you?
B: Very well, thank you. And you?
A: I'm fine too.

Lesson 2

WHO IS HE

A: How do you do? My name is Xie Wen.
B: I'm Anna. How do you do?
A: Very nice to meet you.
B: Very nice to meet you too.

A: Are you the manager?
B: Oh, no. I'm the secretary. He is the manager.
A: Oh, I'm sorry.
B: That's all right.

A: Good morning, Manager. I'm Anna Lee.
B: Good morning, Miss Lee. Who is she?
A: This is Julia.
C: Julia Levy. I am from the United States.
B: Hello, very glad to meet you.
C: Very glad to meet you too.

A: Good morning, Manager.
B: Good morning, Anna.
A: My name is Julia.
B: Oh, yes. Good morning, Mrs. Julia.
A: Miss, Miss Julia Levy.
B: Oh, I'm sorry, Miss Levy.
A: That's all right.

Lesson 3

MY FRIENDS

A: Hi, Anna. Do you know Yamaguchi?
B: Who is Yamaguchi?
A: My Japanese friend.
B: I'm sorry. I don't know her.

A: Xie Wen, who is that?
B: Yamaguchi.
A: Is she a foreign student too?
B: Yes. We are classmates.
A: Are you friends?
B: We are good friends.

A: Hi, Yamaguchi.
B: Hi, Xie Wen.
A: Yamaguchi, let me introduce you to each other. This is Anna.
B: Your friend?
A: Yes, Anna is my friend too.
B: Is she your girl-friend?
A: Anna, what would you say?
C: No, I'm not his girl-friend.
B: I'm not his girl-friend either. Ha ha ha ...
C: Bye-bye.
B: Bye-bye.

Lesson 4

HOW TO CALL A PERSON

A: What's your family name?
B: It's Wan.
A: What's your given name?
B: Wenjie. (My name is) Wan Wenjie.

A: Come in, please.
B: Are you Mr. Gao?
A: Yes, I'm Gao Ya'an. What's your name?
B: My surname is Wan. The full name is Wan Wenjie.
A: Oh, Mr. Wan, sit down, please.
B: Thanks.

A: May I ask your (honorable) name?
B: Not honorable, but my name is Wan, Wan Wenjie.
A: Oh, it's Mr. Wan. Very pleased to meet you.
B: Very pleased to meet you too.

Lesson 5

MAKING TELEPHONE CALLS

A: Hello. This is 54972143.
B: Hello. Is Mrs. Xie in?

A: You've got the wrong number.
B: I'm sorry.

A: Hello. This is Aiyou Company.
B: Hello. Is Mr. Gao Ya'an in?
A: He is not in. Can I help?
B: Oh, please ask him to call me back.
A: Your phone number is ... ?
B: 68370641.
A: OK. Bye-bye.

A: Hello, is that 68370641?
B: That's right. This is Wan Wenjie.
A: This is Gao Ya'an.
B: I phoned you and you were not in.
A: How can I help you?
B: Do you have Mrs. Xie's telephone number?
A: Yes. It's 64960057.
B: Good. Thanks.

Lesson 6

BOOKING A ROOM

A: Hello. This is the reception of Beijing Hotel.
B: I would like to book a room.
A: A suite?

B: No. A standard (double) room.
A: When will you be arriving?
B: Tomorrow.
A: What is your name, please.
B: My name is Wang.
A: We will be expecting your arrival.

A: Miss, I would like to have a room, please.
B: Did you book it beforehand?
A: Yes, I made the booking yesterday by phone.
B: What's your name, please?
A: My name is Wang.
B: Just a moment. Room 3072. Will that do?
A: That's fine. Thank you.
B: You're welcome.

Lesson 7

CHANGING MONEY

A: Miss, we would like to change some money.
B: Cash or traveler's checks?
A: Cash.
C: Mine are traveler's checks.
B: How much do you want to change?
A: What's the exchange rate for today?
B: 100 US dollars to 823.90 RMB yuan.

A: Fine. I'll change 500 US dollars. Will you change some?
C: I won't.

A: Miss, I changed 500 US dollars just now.
B: Is there anything wrong?
A: Today's rate is 100 US dollars to 823.90 RMB yuan. Is that right?
B: That's right.
A: Then 500 US is changed to 4219.50 RMB?
B: It's 4119.50 RMB yuan, Mister, not 4219.50.
A: Oh, I got it wrong. I'm sorry.
B: That's OK.

Lesson 8

TAXI

A: Taxi!
B: Mister, get on, please.
A: To Beijing Hotel.
B: Take you seat.
A: Please stop for a moment when you get to the Friendship Store.
B: OK.

A: Are you on a tour?
B: No, I'm on business.

A: Have you just arrived in Beijing?
B: Yes, how do you know?
A: I'm a taxi driver.
B: Have we got to the Friendship Store?
A: No, it's the traffic jam.
B: Oh.

A: Here is Beijing Hotel, Mister.
B: How much is it?
A: 48.50 yuan.
B: 48.50 yuan? You didn't overcharge, did you?
A: Mister, look, here is my plate number.
B: 64029. OK, here is fifty yuan.
A: Here is 1.50 yuan change
B: Please make out a receipt.
A: OK.
B: Thank you.
A: Good-bye.

Lesson 9

HE HAS NOT TURNED UP FOR WORK

A: Xiao Wang, get the car ready for me, please.
B: When should it be ready?
A: In half an hour.
B: OK.

A: Hello, is Master Zhang there?
B: No, he's not in.
A: Where is he?
B: He has not turned up for work.
A: Oh, thanks.

A: Hello. This is the general reception of the hotel.
B: Hello. This is Aiyou Company. We would like to have a car.
A: When do you want it?
B: 9:45.
A: That is in fifteen minutes, right?
B: Yes. Is that OK?
A: No problem.
B: Thank you.

A: Manager, the car has been arranged.
B: Thank you.
A: You are to get on at the gate of the hotel in fifteen minutes.
B: Is Master Zhang driving?
A: No, Master Zhang is absent today. It is a car from the hotel.
B: All right. That's fine.

Lesson 10

IT IS HER BIRTHDAY TODAY

A: Oh, what beautiful flowers!

B: These are for you.
A: For me? Miss, you...
B: I bought them for you.
A: But I didn't ask you to buy flowers.
B: Hello. Oh, that's Mrs. Qian calling. Yes, he's in. Just a moment. Manager, you are wanted on the phone.

A: Hello, darling, what's the matter?
B: What time is it now?
A: Six o'clock sharp.
B: Aren't you coming home yet?
A: Oh, I'm sorry. I've got an appointment this evening.
B: Have you forgot what day is today?
A: Friday, October 30.
B: Who asked you that?

A: Xiao Wang, my wife just called me and she seemed to be very angry.
B: Why?
A: She asked me what day today is.
B: What did you say?
A: I said that it was October 30, Friday.
B: And your wife hung up?
A: Yes. Did I give the wrong date?
B: No, you didn't.
A: Why was she angry then?
B: It is your wife's birthday today, my great manager.
A: Oh, my God. Thank you for the flowers you bought. And please cancel my appointment.

Lesson 11

WHAT DO YOU WANT TO DO (1)

(In class)
Professor Wang: Hello, everybody. Do you all know one another?
Jack: Let me introduce myself first.
Yamaguchi: There is no need. I know that you are Jack from the United States.
Jack: And I know that you are Yamaguchi from Japan.
Jenny: We all konw one another.
Yamaguchi: I also know that Jenny has come to China to learn Chinese.
Jenny: Do you know why I am learning Chinese?
Yamaguchi: That goes without saying. You learn Chinese so that you can do business in China later.
Jenny: Yes and no.
Jack: What do you mean?
Jenny: Jack, let me ask you why you are learning Chinese.
Jack: I like to make friends.
Jenny: What about you, Yamaguchi?
Yamaguchi: Me? I like to have fun. How can I travel in China if I don't learn Chinese?

Professor Wang: Now, class. You all said that you knew

	Jenny, didn't you?
Jack:	Yes, we all know her.
Professor Wang:	Do you know her well?
Jenny:	No, we don't know one another well enough.
Yamaguchi:	Jack and I don't quite understand what Jenny said just now.
Professor Wang:	Jenny, isn't it for doing business that you are learning Chinese?
Jenny:	To be a shop attendant is also doing business.
Jack:	You don't want to be an attendant, do you?
Jenny:	No.
Yamaguchi:	What about a secretary?
Jenny:	No.
Jack:	What do you want to do then?

Lesson 12

WHAT DO YOU WANT TO DO (2)

(Out of class)

Attendant:	Welcome, welcome. Please come in.
Manager Liu:	How are you, Professor Wang?
Professor Wang:	You are...?
Manager Liu:	You don't recognize me, Professor Wang? I'm Liu Liang, your former student.
Professor Wang:	Oh, it's you, Liu Liang. Have you also come to enjoy yourself?

Manager Liu:	No, I'm the manager of this bar.
Professor Wang:	Oh yeah? I remember you have worked only for three years, and now you are already a manager?
Manager Liu:	You forgot that I studied business management, professor?
Professor Wang:	No, I didn't. You worked hard and studied well.
Manager Liu:	Professor Wang, what would you like to drink? Please make yourselves at home.
Professor Wang:	Anything, tea, Coca Cola, or orange juice?
Jack:	I would like a beer.
Manager Liu:	Fine. Attendant!
Jenny:	Mr. Liu, is it true that you have become a manager only after three years' working experience?
Manager Liu:	Yes, it's true.
Jack:	Jenny, you also want to become a manager of a bar?
Jenny:	Why, can't I? I want to be a boss or a president even.
Jack:	Of course it's all right, but...
Jenny:	But what?
Jack:	You have to come here to be an attendant first.
Jenny:	Why?
Jack:	One should learn how to walk before learning how to run.

Yamaguchi: Jenny can run before learning how to walk, ha...

Lesson 13

DO YOU SPEAK CHINESE (1)

(In class)
Professor Wang: Class, who among you can speak Chinese?
Jack: I can, but I don't speak it well.
Jenny: I have just started learning Chinese, and I can just speak a little.
Professor Wang: I didn't mean that, for I know you all speak a little Chinese.
Jenny: What did you mean then, professor?
Professor Wang: Let me give you a test first. How do you ask for help?
Jenny: All right, let me try.

Jenny: Hey, old chap, where is Beijing University?
Jack: Hey, whose name is Hey? Don't you know how to address people?
Jenny: Oh, I'm sorry. Grandpa, could you tell me where Beijing University is?
Professor Wang: That's right. The old man will tell you gladly now.
Jack: Yes, one should be polite when asking for

	help.
Professor Wang:	Let's try again.
Yamaguchi:	Driver, go to the Great Wall Hotel.
Taxi Driver:	I'm not going.
Yamaguchi:	Hey, why are you going away?
Jack:	Of course he would go away. Who let you call him "Driver"?
Yamaguchi:	What should I call him then?
Jack:	You should call him SHIFU (Master). "SHIFU, I'm going to the Great Wall Hotel."
Yamaguchi:	That's right. You are being so polite and how could the driver possibly be annoyed?
Professor Wang:	Now do you understand what I mean by that question?
Jenny:	Yes, I do.

Lesson 14

DO YOU SPEAK CHINESE (2)

(Out of class)

Jenny: Jack, the Chinese lesson yesterday was very interesting indeed.

Jack: You are right. It is really not easy to speak Chinese

well.
Jenny: Let's have some more practice together.
Jack: Fine. I'll play the shop assistant, and you the customer. How about that?
Jenny: Good. Let's begin.

Jack: Miss, welcome you to come and buy things.
Jenny: Welcome me to buy things. Will it not do if I have just come to have a look round and don't buy anything?
Jack: Oh, welcome. Do as you please.
Jenny: Look, you didn't say the right thing and the customer was angry.
Jack: OK, let's try again.

Jack: Miss, what do you want?
Jenny: What the hell did you say? Have I come to ask for things?
Jack: I didn't mean that, please don't misunderstand me.
Jenny: Did I misunderstand you, or you didn't say the right thing?
Jack: Oh, I'm sorry.

Jack: Look, I got it wrong again.
Jenny: You couldn't say: "What do you want?"
Jack: What should I say then?
Jenny: You should say: "Miss, what do you intend to buy?"
Jack: No, that's not right. "I don't want to buy

	anything. Will it not do if I just have a look round?"
Jenny:	Mm. The customer would also get angry if you said that.
Jack:	What should I say then?
Jenny:	Oh, it's too difficult. I don't know what to say either.

Lesson 15

DO YOU KNOW HOW TO MAKE PURCHASES (1)

(In class)

Professor Wang:	Class, do you know how to make purchases?
Jenny:	Yes, I give them the cash and get the goods.
Jack:	That simple?
Professor Wang:	You can have a try and see whether it is that simple.
Jack:	Hey, how much is a *jin* of these apples?
Jenny:	Jack, don't buy here.
Jack:	Why? You don't know how to beat the seller down?
Jenny:	Not that I don't know how, but we can't do it here.
Jack:	Why?

Jenny:	This apple seller is the father of a friend of mine.
Jenny:	Hello, how much is a *jin* of these apples?
Peddler:	Three *jin* for twelve yuan.
Jenny:	Three *jin* for ten yuan, OK?
Peddler:	Ten yuan for two and half *jin*.
Jenny:	What? That is still four yuan a *jin*.
Jack:	My little boss, you are really capable of cheating.
Jenny:	Three *jin* for ten yuan. If you don't agree, we'll go.
Peddler:	OK, OK. Ten yuan for three *jin*.
Jenny:	How was that? I beat him down by two yuan.
Jack:	How many *jin* of apples did you buy?
Jenny:	Three.
Jack:	Go and have them weighed, and they weigh at most two and half *jin*.
Jenny:	Really? That is still four yuan a *jin*.
Jack:	What do you think? Making purchases is not as simple as you think.

Lesson 16

DO YOU KNOW HOW TO MAKE PURCHESE (2)

(Out of class)

Jenny: Jack, do you like reading advertisements?
Jack: I don't, but I have to.
Jenny: Why?
Jack: How can you buy things without reading ads?
Jenny: And you know how to make purchases after reading ads?
Jack: Of course. If you don't believe, we can have a try.
Jenny: Then, ... let's go and buy a watermelon.
Jack: Let's go.

Jenny: Jack, please have a look at the words written on this small blackboard.
Jack: One *jin* for 1.50 yuan. Authentic American Watermelon 118, with the shortcoming being too sweet.
Jenny: American watermelon sold in China. Have you ever tasted it?
Jack: No, not yet.
Jenny: What do you think? Shall we buy some?
Jack: Yes, the watermelon is sweet and I like sweet melons.

Jack: How much a *jin* are these melons?
Peddler: 1.50 yuan for one *jin*.
Jack: That's too expensive. Could you make it a bit cheaper?
Peddler: No, I can't. This is authentic American 118.
Jack: What is written on the small blackboard is not

	deceptive, is it?
Peddler:	How can it be?
Jack:	Good. Little boss, choose one for me.
Peddler:	OK.
Jack:	How much is it?
Peddler:	It's 11 *jin* and half. That's 17.25 yuan. Let's make it 17 yuan.
Jack:	Please cut a small piece (and let's have a look).
Peddler:	OK.
Jack:	Little boss, how come that the melon is not sweet at all?
Peddler:	It is clearly written here. Its shortcoming is too sweet. Then its merit is that it is not sweet.
Jack:	Oh, this ad of yours...
Jenny:	What would you say, Jack? Ads can be deceptive too.

Lesson 17

WHAT'S THE MATTER WITH HER (1)

(In class)

Professor Wang:	Good morning, class.
Students:	Good morning, Professor.
Professor Wang:	Is everybody here?
Jenny,	Anna and Jack aren't here.
Professor Wang:	Anything the matter with them?
Jenny:	Anna is ill, and Jack has accompanied her to

	the hospital.
Professor Wang:	What's wrong with her?
Jenny:	Perhaps she's caught a cold. She said that she was not feeling well.
Professor Wang:	Was she running a fever? Has she had her temperature taken?
Jenny:	Yes. 38.5 degrees Celsius.
Professor Wang:	Oh, that's quite high. Did she have a cough?
Jenny:	No, and her throat wasn't sore either. But she was feeling thirsty.
Professor Wang:	She should drink plenty of water.
Jenny:	That won't do, for she had diarrhea.
Professor Wang:	In that case, she should drink even more water.
Jenny:	Won't that aggravate her diarrhea?
Professor Wang:	Oh, no, it won't.
Yamaguchi:	I think that may not be a cold. Perhaps she ate something bad.
Professor Wang:	Now let's begin our class. We'll go and see her after class.

Lesson 18

WHAT'S THE MATTER WITH HER (2)

(Out of class)

Qian Fucheng:	Mister, are you on a tour?
Jack:	Yes, what about you?
Qian Fucheng:	I am on a business trip, traveling for commercial purposes.
Jack:	Doing business? Why don't you travel by air?
Qian Fucheng:	To save some money by bearing hardships.
Jack:	But traveling by train is too slow. Businessmen pay most attention to time.
Qian Fucheng:	That's right. Time is money.
Jack:	But...
Qian Fucheng:	It doesn't matter. It's a general holiday today.
Jack:	That's right. Nobody would be at work today.
Qian Fucheng:	How come that your friend is sleeping all the way?
Jack:	She has been ill for several days. I asked her not to come, but she insisted on coming.
Qian Fucheng:	Why is she just sleeping without taking some medicine?
Jack:	We forgot to bring them, and we want to buy some when we get off the train.
Qian Fucheng:	Oh, please wait a minute and I'll send for a doctor.
Qian Fucheng:	The doctor is here.
Doctor:	What's wrong with you, Miss?
Anna:	I had loose bowels during the last few days. Now the diarrhea has stopped, but I have a terrible headache.
Doctor:	Oh, you are running a fever. Let me take your

	temperature.
Anna:	What's wrong with me?
Doctor:	Give me the thermometer, please. 40 degrees Celsius. That's too high. Let me have a look at your throat.
Jack:	Anything wrong?
Doctor:	The throat has become inflamed.
Jack:	Does she need an injection? She is afraid of that.
Doctor:	Let her take some antipyretics first, once every four hours, two tablets each time.
Anna:	Doctor, is it serious?
Doctor:	Go and have a thorough check-up in the hospital when you get off the train.
Anna:	Oh, my God. Don't let me be hospitalized.

Lesson 19

WHOSE FAULT IS IT (1)

(In class)

Jack:	Good morning, Professor.
Professor Wang:	Good morning. Why are you late again today?
Jack:	But I am not late! Look, my watch says it's 7:50. Actually I've come early.
Jenny:	7:50? It's already 8:15. You're fifteen minutes late.

Jack: How could that be? Your watch must be wrong.

Professor Wang: All right. Sit down and take out your book please.

Jack: Oh, too bad.

Jenny: You have brought the wrong book again, haven't you?

Jack: Isn't this the listening comprehension class by Professor Zhang? How come this is Professor Wang's oral class?

Jenny: This is Professor Wang's oral class.

Jack: I felt odd when I entered the classroom a moment ago. What day is today?

Jenny: It's Tuesday today.

Jack: Tuesday? Look, today is Monday according to my watch.

Jenny: I was wondering why you didn't come to class yesterday. Now I see. You thought yesterday was Sunday.

Jack: But I didn't take a rest. I was working to earn some money.

Professor Wang: What were you two talking about?

Jenny: Jack thought it was Monday today, and he has only brought the book for listening comprehension.

Jack: Professor, I'm not to blame. It's my watch that is wrong. I guarantee that it won't be

Yamaguchi:	wrong again tomorrow. Who's to blame then if you are late again for class tomorrow?
Jack:	Yes, who should be blamed then? Myself? Oh, no...

Lesson 20

WHOSE FAULT IS IT (2)

(Out of class)

Jack:	(Excuse me,) Miss, what time is Express No. 14 from Shanghai arriving?
Miss:	Express No. 14 should be arriving at one minute past nine. It's only half past seven now. It's too early.
Jack:	What? Only half past seven?
Miss:	Yes. You see the clock on the tall building says it's half past seven now.
Jack:	No. I've just set my watch. It's now half past eight. The clock on that tall building must be slow.
Miss:	How could that be? It's your watch that is fast.
Jack:	Is it? This damn watch made me get up very early, and now I have to wait for more than one hour.
Miss:	Have you come to meet somebody?

Jack: Yes, to meet a friend of mine from Shanghai.
Miss: Is this your friend's first visit to Beijing?
Jack: No, he often comes to Beijing by train on business. It's my first time to come to the railway station.
Miss: Oh, in that case, it's your friend who should have come to meet you.
Jack: Why?
Miss: Because he wouldn't have said that the clock on that tall building was wrong.

Jack: Hi, Steven, I'm here!
Steven: Hi, Jack, nice to meet you.
Jack: Was it a smooth trip?
Steven: Everything's fine.
Jack: Everything is always fine for you, but I often run into trouble.
Steven: What was wrong?
Jack: This damn watch of mine always holds things up.
Steven: What's wrong with your watch?
Jack: It was slow during the last few days so that I was late for class several times. Today it is fast and makes me wait for you here for more than one hour.
Steven: Ha... You will be fired if you are an employee in my company.

Lesson 21

WHERE ARE YOU STAYING (1)

(In class)
Professor Wang: Jack, where are you staying?
Jack: In Building No. 4 of our university.
Professor Wang: What about you, Jenny?
Jenny: Also in Building No. 4.
Professor Wang: In which room then?
Jenny: On the third floor, Room 347. And Jack's on the second floor, Room 215.
Professor Wang: Is there a telephone in your room?
Jack: No, but there is a public phone in the corridor.
Yamaguchi: That's inconvenient.
Jenny: Yes, it is. I am quite far from the phone and I often can't hear it.
Jack: Sometimes there are many people waiting to use the phone, and you have to queue up for a long time.
Jenny: Yamaguchi is lucky, for she has a phone in her home.

Professor Wang: Where do you live, Yamaguchi?
Yamaguchi: Near the Asian Games Village, not far from the university.
Professor Wang: Why don't you stay in the university?

Jack: It is very expensive to live outside the university.

Yamaguchi: The firm my husband works for has rented an apartment for us, and we don't have to pay the rent.

Jack: How's the environment?

Yamaguchi: Very good. It's very convenient whether you want to go shopping or for recreation.

Jenny: Oh, that's superb.

Yamaguchi: You are all welcome to visit my home. This is my husband's card, with the address and telephone number on it.

Jenny: Thank you. We would really like to come and visit you when we have time.

Lesson 22

WHERE ARE YOU STAYING (2)

(Out of class)

Jenny: Hi, Yamaguchi. Fancy meeting you here.

Yamaguchi: Indeed, it's a nice surprise.

Jack: Yamaguchi, what do you intend to buy?

Yamaguchi: I have come for some electrical household appliances.

Jenny: Isn't the apartment at the Asian Games Village

	equipped with TV, fridge and washing machine?
Yamaguchi:	Yes. But I would like to have a home cinema.
Jenny:	Oh, that would cost a fortune.
Yamaguchi:	Yes, could you help me with the selection?
Jenny:	OK, let's go together.
Shop Assistant:	Miss, your patronage to our store is most welcome.
Yamaguchi:	Could you introduce your goods to us?
Shop Assistant:	What do you intend to buy, Miss?
Yamaguchi:	I'd like a few electrical home appliances.
Shop Assistant:	Fine, please follow me.
Yamaguchi:	Do you deliver to domicile?
Shop Assistant:	Yes, we do it free of charge.
Jack:	Which door do you deliver goods to? The door of the building or the door of the apartment?
Jenny:	I hear that delivery to domicile here means delivering to the gate of the building.
Yamaguchi:	And I live on 22nd floor.
Shop Assistant:	Please rest assured. We guarantee to deliver the goods to your apartment on the 22nd floor.
Yamaguchi:	Do you make prompt delivery right after my purchase?
Shop Assistant:	Where do you live, Miss?
Yamaguchi:	At the Asian Games Village.
Shop Assistant:	The Asian Games Village is too far away from our store. I am afraid it may take one week to have the goods delivered.

Yamaguchi: It takes that long? Can't you do it right away?
Shop Assistant: I am afraid not. Our store does not serve you alone. We can't manage it.
Jack: Yamaguchi, let's go and find a store that's near the Asian Games Village.
Jenny: Let's go. If the store does not want to earn the moeny, we do not want to make our purchase here either.
Shop Assistant: Oh, Miss. Please buy them here. We will make delivery immediately.

Lesson 23

WHAT'S THE WEATHER LIKE TODAY (1)

(In class)
Jack: How is today, Anna?
Anna: I feel fine today.
Jack: I already know that you've recovered and are enjoying good health.
Anna: Then what were you asking about?
Jack: I was asking about what the weather was like today.
Anna: Mm, ... it looks fine to me.
Jack: What is the highest air temperature?

Anna:	I don't know.
Jack:	Didn't you listen to the weather forecast?
Anna:	How could I understand?
Jack:	Let's go and ask our professor then.

Anna:	Professor Wang, how can we understand the weather forecast?
Professor Wang:	Oh, that's easy. I happen to have the recording of today's weather forecast with me here. You can listen to it.
Anna:	That's terrific.

Hello, dear listeners. We are now broadcasting the weather forecast for the cities in the next 24 hours. For Beijing, it will be turning from cloudy to overcast tonight. There will be light rain mingled with snow. The low will be minus 7 (degrees Celsius). During the daytime tomorrow, it will be turning from cloudy to clear. There will be a force 2 to 3 wind (on the Beaufort scale). The high will be 2 (degrees Celsius).

Professor Wang:	Do you understand?
Jack:	Just a little.
Anna:	I don't understand a bit of it.
Professor Wang:	Don't worry. If you listen to it more often, you will surely be able to understand.

Lesson 24

WHAT'S THE WEATHER LIKE TODAY (2)

(Out of class)
Jenny: Jack, look, it looks like rain.
Jack: Didn't you say that the weather forecast said that it would not rain today?
Yamaguchi: Jenny said that it would be fine today.
Jenny: The weather forecast said exactly that. How come that the weather has changed without any warning?
Jack: Our teacher said that Beijing's weather is noted for the rain in summer, snow in winter and wind in spring.
Yamaguchi: Autumn is the best season in Beijing, with no wind and little rain, being neither cold nor hot.
Jenny: I forgot what our teacher said. It is the rainy season now and we have to take our raincoats with us when going out.
Yamaguchi: And we are riding our bicycles. How can we go back to the university then?
Jack: I know what to do. Please follow me.

Jack: Miss, we are caught in the rain and we have forgot to bring our rain gear. Can you lend it to us?
Miss: Of course. What would you like, umbrella or

	raincoat?
Jack:	We are riding our bicycles and we prefer raincoats.
Miss:	That's fine.
Jack:	When do we have to return them?
Miss:	You can bring them back when you come to the store next time.
Jack:	Do we have to return them to this store?
Miss:	Oh, no. There are a dozen shops in this city that offer this service. You can send them to a shop that's nearest to your place.
Jack:	Thank you.
Jenny:	Jack, you seem to know that young lady very well.
Jack:	No, I don't know her at all.
Jenny:	Then how do you know that she would lend rain gear to you?
Jack:	My Chinese friends told me that I could borrow rain gear from stores.
Yamaguchi:	Aren't they afraid that the borrowers would not return them?
Jack:	Courtesy umbrellas are for the use of the public, and they trust that everybody pays attention to civilized conducts.

Lesson 25

ROAMING AROUND BEIJING (1)

(In class)

Professor Wang: Hello, everybody. How long have you been in Beijing now?
Jack: It has been almost a year since I came to Beijing.
Jenny: For me it's less than half a year.
Professor Wang: Have you roamed around Beijing yet?
Jack: Jenny and I did it quite often.
Professor Wang: What about Yamaguchi?
Yamaguchi: I went downtown several times by taxi.
Jack: You call that roaming around? You should go on bike.
Yamaguchi: I don't know the way. I am afraid I can't find my way home if I go by bike.
Jenny: Why not ask someone to lead the way?
Yamaguchi: Who should I ask then?
Jack: Me. I am already a veteran of Beijing.

Professor Wang: Jack, you said that you were already a veteran of Beijing?
Jack: Well, that's embarrassing. I was just cracking a joke.
Professor Wang: Do you know Beijing well?
Jack: I can't say I do. But I won't get lost if I go

	downtown by bike.
Professor Wang:	What's your trick then?
Jack:	That's simple. Beijing's streets, lanes and roads are all straight, either going north and south, or east and west.
Jenny:	As long as one remembers the location of our university, one won't lose the way.
Yamaguchi:	That won't do. I can't orient myself.
Jack:	There is another way. Just remember turning left, and then right...
Yamaguchi:	No, no, one turn after another will surely get me confused.
Jenny:	Yamaguchi, then you'd better spend money to hire a taxi. You will not get confused in a taxi. Ha, ha ha...

Lesson 26

ROAMING AROUND BEIJING (2)

(Out of class)

Yamaguchi:	Jack, where are we off to?
Jack:	First to Wangfujing, then to Dashilan at Qianmen and Xidan.
Yamaguchi:	Why to these places?
Jenny:	Because they are the three most bustling business streets in Beijing.

Yamaguchi:	Good, let's go. I'll follow you two.
Jack:	In front of us is Wangfujing. Let's park our bikes here, and it will be easy for us to collect them when we leave.
Yamaguchi:	Oh, it's really a bustling scene. There are so many shops here, one next to another.
Jenny:	Listen, what is the man over there crying out?

"Please stop to have a look. Export goods for domestic sale." "Fantastic beauty cream. Excellent cosmetic for ladies. Buy two for the price of one."

Jack:	I don't quite understand him. It sounds like he's urging you to stop and buy his stuff.
Yamaguchi:	Let's go and have a look.
Jack:	Here is North Xidan Street.
Yamaguchi:	It is different here from Dashilan, but similar to Wangfujing.
Jenny:	Dashilan is a traditional business street, narrow with antique shop fronts.
Jack:	Both Xidan and Wangfujing are modern business streets with magnificent tall buildings.
Jenny:	In these stores, you can buy almost anything that's available anywhere in the world.
Yamaguchi:	Really? Is all the merchandise imported?
Jack:	No, imported or domestic, everything is being sold here, and everything is being bought here.

Jenny: China is really populous, with lots of shops and lots of goods. Whatever is offered for sale is being bought. It's easy to do business and make money here.

Yamaguchi: Judging by the way you spoke, you seemed to have earned a lot of money on the Chinese market.

Jack: Ha, Congratulations and may you be prosperous!

Jenny: The same to you!

生词总表
Vocabulary List

A

啊 à ……………………… 2
哎呀 āiyā …………… 19
挨 āi ………………… 26
爱 ài ………………… 11
爱人 àiren …………… 3
安排 ānpái …………… 9
安全带 ānquándài ……… 8

B

八 bā ………………… 5
把 bǎ ………………… 18
爸爸 bàba …………… 1
吧 ba ………………… 8
白天 báitiān ………… 23
百 bǎi ………………… 7
拜访 bàifǎng ………… 21
半 bàn ………………… 9
办法 bànfǎ …………… 24
办公室 bàngōngshì …… 5

帮助 bāngzhù ………… 13
保证 bǎozhèng ……… 19
杯 bēi ………………… 12
北 běi ………………… 25
北京 Běijīng …………… 6
本店 běndiàn ………… 22
本市 běnshì …………… 24
笔直 bǐzhí …………… 25
比 bǐ ………………… 7
比价 bǐjià …………… 7
必须 bìxū …………… 24
边 biān ……………… 21
变 biàn ……………… 24
遍 biàn ……………… 23
标准间 biāozhǔnjiān …… 6
别 bié ………………… 6
别人 biérén …………… 13
冰箱 bīngxiāng ……… 22
病 bìng ……………… 17
播送 bōsòng ………… 23
不 bù ………………… 2
不过 bùguò …………… 12

C

才 cái ·············· 13
彩色 cǎisè ·········· 22
层 céng ············· 22
茶 chá ·············· 12
差 chà ··············· 9
差不多 chàbuduō ······ 26
长 cháng ············ 22
长城 Chángchéng ····· 13
常 cháng ············ 20
潮湿 cháoshī ········ 24
吵架 chǎojià ········ 24
车 chē ·············· 8
称 chēng ············ 15
称呼 chēnghu ········· 4
城市 chéngshì ······· 23
吃 chī ·············· 16
迟到 chídào ········· 19
抽烟 chōuyān ········ 15
出差 chūchāi ········ 18
出口 chūkǒu ········· 26
出来 chūlái ········· 19
出门 chūmén ········· 24
出租车 chūzū chē ····· 8
传统 chuántǒng ······ 26
春天 chūntiān ······· 24
次 cì ··············· 20
从 cóng ············· 20
存 cún ·············· 26
错 cuò ··············· 5

D

打 dǎ ················ 5
打的 dǎdī ············ 8
打工 dǎgōng ········· 19
打针 dǎzhēn ········· 18
大 dà ··············· 10
大家 dàjiā ·········· 11
大街 dàjiē ·········· 25
大名 dàmíng ·········· 4
大娘 dàniáng ········ 13
大厦 dàshà ·········· 26
大学 dàxué ·········· 13
大爷 dàye ··········· 17
大夫 dàifu ·········· 18
带 dài ·············· 18
带路 dàilù ·········· 25
单人间 dānrén jiān ··· 6
耽误 dānwu ·········· 20
但是 dànshì ········· 13
蛋糕 dàngāo ········· 10
当 dāng ············· 11
当然 dāngrán ········ 12
到 dào ··············· 8
到底 dàodǐ ·········· 25

295

倒是 dàoshì …… 26	兑换 duìhuàn …… 7
的 de …… 3	多少 duōshao …… 7
得 de …… 12	
得体 détǐ …… 14	**E**
得 děi …… 12	
等 děng …… 6	俄罗斯 Éluósī …… 2
低 dī …… 17	二 èr …… 5
地方 dìfang …… 25	
地址 dìzhǐ …… 21	**F**
弟弟 dìdi …… 1	
第 dì …… 20	发财 fācái …… 26
点 diǎn …… 7	地票 fāpiào …… 8
点 diǎn …… 9	发烧 fāshāo …… 17
电话 diànhuà …… 5	发炎 fāyán …… 18
电器 diànqì …… 22	法国 Fǎguó …… 2
电视 diànshì …… 22	繁华 fánhuá …… 26
电影院 diànyǐngyuàn …… 22	饭店 fàndiàn …… 6
掉 diào …… 15	方便 fāngbiàn …… 21
丢 diū …… 25	方向 fāngxiàng …… 25
东 dōng …… 25	芳名 fāngmíng …… 4
东西 dōngxi …… 14	房间 fángjiān …… 6
冬天 dōngtiān …… 24	房租 fángzū …… 21
懂 dǒng …… 23	放心 fàngxīn …… 22
都 dōu …… 11	飞机 fēijī …… 18
堵车 dǔchē …… 8	分 fēn …… 7
度 dù …… 17	分 fēn …… 9
肚子 dùzi …… 17	分 fēn …… 5
对 duì …… 2	风力 fēnglì …… 23
对不起 duìbuqǐ …… 2	夫人 fūren …… 2

服务 fúwù	24	古色古香 gǔsègǔxiāng	26
服务台 fúwùtái	6	顾客 gùkè	14
服务员 fúwùyuán	11	挂 guà	10
付 fù	21	拐 guǎi	25
附近 fùjìn	21	怪 guài	19
		管 guǎn	22
G		管理 guǎnlǐ	12
		光 guāng	18
干燥 gānzào	24	光临 guānglín	6
感冒 gǎnmào	17	广告 guǎnggào	16
刚 gāng	8	逛 guàng	25
刚才 gāngcái	7	贵 guì	4
高烧 gāoshāo	18	贵 guì	16
高兴 gāoxìng	2	国 guó	2
告诉 gàosu	13	国际 guójì	8
哥哥 gēge	1	过 guò	9
个 gè	6		
各地 gèdì	26	**H**	
给 gěi	5		
跟 gēn	22	哈 hā	3
更 gèng	17	嗨 hāi	1
工作 gōngzuò	12	还 hái	10
公里 gōnglǐ	8	还是 háishì	7
公司 gōngsī	5	害 hài	20
公用 gōngyòng	21	韩国 Hánguó	2
公寓 gōngyù	21	汉语 Hànyǔ	11
恭候 gōnghòu	6	好 hǎo	1
恭喜 gōngxǐ	26	好像 hǎoxiàng	10
购物 gòuwù	14	号码 hàomǎ	5

嗬 hē ... 26	记得 jìde ... 12
喝 hē ... 12	季节 jìjié ... 24
和 hé ... 11	家 jiā ... 10
黑板 hēibǎn ... 16	家庭 jiātíng ... 22
很 hěn ... 1	佳品 jiāpǐn ... 26
后天 hòutiān ... 6	价格 jiàgé ... 15
呼 hū ... 5	简单 jiǎndān ... 15
胡同 hútòngr ... 25	检查 jiǎnchá ... 18
糊涂 hútu ... 25	件 jiàn ... 22
互相 hùxiāng ... 11	贱 jiàn ... 4
华氏 huáshì ... 17	讲究 jiǎngjiu ... 18
话 huà ... 11	交 jiāo ... 11
化妆 huàzhuāng ... 26	角 jiǎo ... 7
坏 huài ... 17	叫 jiào ... 4
欢迎 huānyíng ... 12	教室 jiàoshì ... 5
还 huán ... 24	接 jiē ... 20
环境 huánjìng ... 21	节 jié ... 19
换 huàn ... 7	节省 jiéshěng ... 18
回 huí ... 10	姐姐 jiějie ... 1
会 huì ... 12	借 jiè ... 24
汇率 huìlǜ ... 7	介绍 jièshào ... 3
惠顾 huìgù ... 22	斤 jīn ... 15
火车 huǒchē ... 18	今天 jīntiān ... 6
货 huò ... 15	金钱 jīnqián ... 18
	进 jìn ... 4
J	进口 jìnkǒu ... 26
	经费 jīngfèi ... 18
几 jǐ ... 18	经济 jīngjì ... 12
系 jì ... 8	经理 jīnglǐ ... 2

九 jiǔ	5	课本 kèběn	19
久仰 jiǔyǎng	4	肯 kěn	24
酒 jiǔ	12	恐怕 kǒngpà	22
酒吧 jiǔbā	12	口 kǒu	17
就是 jiùshì	9	口气 kǒuqì	26
橘汁 júzhī	12	口语 kǒuyǔ	19
橘子 júzi	15	口子 kǒuzi	16
句 jù	13	苦 kǔ	18
觉得 juéde	19	块 kuài	7
		快 kuài	20
K		矿泉水 kuàngquánshuǐ	12
咖啡 kāfēi	12	**L**	
开 kāi	8	拉 lā	17
开车 kāichē	9	啦 la	10
开除 kāichú	16	来 lái	6
开始 kāishǐ	13	劳驾 láojià	13
砍 kǎn	15	老 lǎo	13
看 kàn	8	老板 lǎobǎn	12
考试 kǎoshì	13	老师 lǎoshī	1
看样子 kànyàngzi	23	老头 lǎotóu	13
咳嗽 késou	17	了 le	6
可口可乐 Kěkǒu Kělè	12	冷 lěng	24
可能 kěnéng	17	离 lí	21
可是 kěshì	11	里 lǐ	21
可以 kěyǐ	6	礼貌 lǐmào	13
渴 kě	17	立即 lìjí	22
客气 kèqi	6	厉害 lìhai	18
刻 kè	9		

299

俩 liǎ	19	买进价 mǎijìnjià	7
练习 liànxí	14	卖 mài	15
凉快 liángkuai	24	卖出价 màichūjià	7
量 liáng	17	慢 màn	18
两 liǎng	15	忙 máng	22
辆 liàng	9	没关系 méi guānxi	2
了解 liǎojiě	11	没有 méiyǒu	8
咧 liē	16	美国 Měiguó	2
零 líng	5	美容霜 měiróngshuāng	26
零下 língxià	23	美元 Měiyuán	7
留学生 liúxuéshēng	3	妹妹 mèimei	1
留言 liúyán	5	门口 ménkǒu	9
六 liù	5	门脸 ménliǎn	26
楼 lóu	20	门面 ménmiàn	26
楼道 lóudào	21	们 men	3
路 lù	25	蒙人 mēngrén	15
录音 lùyīn	23	迷 mí	26
旅行 lǚxíng	7	秘书 mìshū	2
啰 luo	16	免 miǎn	4
		免费 miǎnfèi	22
M		面 miàn	21
		名片 míngpiàn	21
妈妈 māma	1	名字 míngzì	4
麻烦 máfan	20	明白 míngbai	11
马路 mǎlù	25	明天 míngtiān	6
马上 mǎshàng	22		
吗 ma	1	**N**	
嘛 ma	18		
买 mǎi	10	嗯 ng	14

拿 ná	19
哪 nǎ	2
哪儿 nǎr	8
哪里 nǎli	23
那 nà	3
那儿 nàr	8
那么 nàme	11
男 nán	3
南 nán	25
难 nán	15
呢 ne	1
内销 nèixiāo	26
能 néng	14
你 nǐ	1
年 nián	10
您 nín	4
努力 nǔlì	12
女 nǚ	3
暖和 nuǎnhuo	24

O

噢 ō	6
哦 ó	7
欧 ōu	8

P

怕 pà	18
跑 pǎo	12
陪 péi	17
朋友 péngyou	3
啤酒 píjiǔ	12
便宜 piányi	16
片 piàn	18
漂亮 piàoliang	10
苹果 píngguǒ	15
瓶 píng	12
葡萄 pútao	15
葡萄酒 pútaojiǔ	12

Q

七 qī	5
欺骗 qīpiàn	16
奇怪 qíguài	19
骑 qí	24
起床 qǐchuáng	20
起价 qǐjià	8
气派 qìpài	26
气温 qìwēn	23
千 qiān	7
前天 qiántiān	6
钱 qián	7
巧 qiǎo	22
亲爱的 qīn'àide	10
清楚 qīngchu	25
晴 qíng	23

请 qǐng ……………… 4	商店 shāngdiàn ………… 8
请假 qǐngjià ………… 17	商品 shāngpǐn ………… 22
请求 qǐngqiú ………… 13	商业 shāngyè ………… 26
秋天 qiūtiān ………… 24	上班 shàngbān ………… 9
取 qǔ ………………… 26	上车 shàngchē ………… 8
取消 qǔxiāo ………… 10	上帝 shàngdì ………… 18
去 qù ………………… 8	上课 shàngkè ………… 17
缺点 quēdiǎn ……… 16	上星期 shàngxīngqī … 10
	摄氏 shèshì …………… 17
R	身体 shēntǐ …………… 23
	什么 shénme ………… 4
然后 ránhòu ………… 26	生气 shēngqì ………… 10
让 ràng ……………… 13	生日 shēngrì ………… 10
热 rè ………………… 24	生意 shēngyi ………… 8
热闹 rènao ………… 26	声 shēng ……………… 13
人 rén ………………… 2	师傅 shīfu …………… 9
人民币 Rénmínbì …… 7	十 shí ………………… 5
认识 rènshi ………… 2	时候 shíhou …………… 6
日 rì ………………… 10	时间 shíjiān ………… 18
日本 Rìběn …………… 2	是 shì ………………… 2
日子 rìzi …………… 10	事 shì ………………… 5
容易 róngyì ………… 14	试 shì ………………… 13
如果 rúguǒ ………… 19	世界 shìjiè …………… 26
	收费 shōufèi ………… 8
S	手 shǒu ……………… 15
	手表 shǒubiǎo ……… 19
三 sān ………………… 5	手机 shǒujī …………… 5
嗓子 sǎngzi ………… 17	售货员 shòuhuòyuán … 14
商场 shāngchǎng …… 24	书 shū ………………… 3

302

舒服 shūfu	17	套间 tàojiān	6
熟 shú	24	特别 tèbié	20
双人间 shuāngrénjiān	6	特点 tèdiǎn	24
双休日 shuāngxiūrì	18	疼 téng	17
谁 shuí	2	体温 tǐwēn	17
水 shuǐ	17	体温表 tǐwēnbiǎo	17
水果 shuǐguǒ	15	替 tì	10
睡觉 shuìjiào	18	天 tiān	10
顺便 shùnbiàn	24	天气 tiānqì	23
顺利 shùnlì	20	甜 tián	16
说 shuō	3	挑选 tiāoxuǎn	16
司机 sījī	8	条 tiáo	26
死 sǐ	20	听 tīng	12
四 sì	5	听力 tīnglì	19
送 sòng	10	听众 tīngzhòng	23
宿舍 sùshè	5	停车 tíngchē	8
算 suàn	7	同事 tóngshì	3
随便 suíbiàn	12	同学 tóngxué	3
岁 suì	15	同志 tóngzhì	13
所以 suǒyǐ	19	退 tuì	18

T

W

他 tā	2	外 wài	21
她 tā	3	玩 wán	11
它 tā	19	玩笑 wánxiào	25
太 tài	11	晚 wǎn	19
太太 tàitai	3	晚点 wǎndiǎn	20
套 tào	21	晚上 wǎnshang	1

303

万 wàn	5
往 wǎng	25
忘 wàng	10
为 wèi	14
为了 wèile	11
为什么 wèi shénme	10
位 wèi	24
喂 wèi	5
文明 wénmíng	24
问 wèn	4
问题 wèntí	7
我 wǒ	1
五 wǔ	5
误会 wùhuì	14

X

西 xī	25
西瓜 xīguā	15
吸毒 xīdú	17
洗衣机 xǐyījī	22
喜欢 xǐhuan	11
下班 xiàbān	9
下车 xiàchē	8
下课 xiàkè	17
下午 xiàwǔ	1
下星期 xiàxīngqī	10
夏天 xiàtiān	24
先 xiān	11

先生 xiānsheng	1
鲜花 xiānhuā	10
现代化 xiàndàihuà	26
现金 xiànjīn	7
现在 xiànzài	9
相信 xiāngxìn	16
香蕉 xiāngjiāo	15
想 xiǎng	11
响 xiǎng	21
向 xiàng	25
项 xiàng	24
小贩 xiǎofàn	15
小姐 xiǎojie	1
小时 xiǎoshí	9
效劳 xiàoláo	14
些 xiē	22
写 xiě	16
谢谢 xièxie	1
星期 xīngqī	10
星期一 xīngqīyī	10
星期二 xīngqī'èr	10
星期三 xīngqīsān	10
星期四 xīngqīsì	10
星期五 xīngqīwǔ	10
星期六 xīngqīliù	10
星期日 xīngqīrì	10
行 xíng	9
姓 xìng	4
幸会 xìnghuì	4

休息 xiūxi	18	以为 yǐwéi	19
学生 xuésheng	2	已经 yǐjīng	9
学习 xuéxí	11	意思 yìsi	11
雪 xuě	23	阴 yīn	23
寻呼台 xúnhūtái	5	银行 yínháng	7
		饮料 yǐnliào	12
		应该 yīnggāi	13
Y		英国 Yīngguó	2
		用 yòng	9
呀 yā	15	优点 yōudiǎn	16
羊肉串 yángròuchuàn	19	邮局 yóujú	8
吆喝 yāohe	26	有 yǒu	5
要 yào	6	有空 yǒukòng	21
要 yào	14	友谊 yǒuyì	8
要紧 yàojǐn	18	又 yòu	14
要是 yàoshì	14	右 yòu	21
药 yào	18	娱乐 yúlè	21
也 yě	1	雨 yǔ	23
一 yī	5	雨具 yǔjù	24
一次 yīcì	18	雨伞 yǔsǎn	24
一点儿 yīdiǎnr	13	雨衣 yǔyī	24
一定 yīdìng	13	遇到 yùdào	20
一共 yīgòng	16	遇上 yùshàng	22
一路 yīlù	18	预报 yùbào	23
一起 yīqǐ	14	预订 yùdìng	6
一切 yīqiè	20	元 yuán	7
一下 yīxià	3	原来 yuánlái	19
医院 yīyuàn	17	远 yuǎn	21
以后 yǐhòu	9	约会 yuēhuì	10
以前 yǐqián	11		

305

月 yuè	10
云 yún	23

Z

在 zài	5
再 zài	13
再见 zàijiàn	3
糟糕 zāogāo	19
早 zǎo	19
早上 zǎoshang	1
怎么 zěnme	4
怎么样 zěnmeyàng	15
占线 zhànxiàn	5
站 zhàn	20
张 zhāng	8
着急 zháojí	23
找 zhǎo	8
这 zhè	2
这么 zhème	20
这样 zhèyàng	13
着 zhe	16
真 zhēn	12
整 zhěng	9
正点 zhèngdiǎn	20
正好 zhènghǎo	23
正在 zhèngzài	11
正宗 zhèngzōng	16
挣 zhèng	19
知道 zhīdao	5
支票 zhīpiào	7
职员 zhíyuán	20
只 zhǐ	13
中国 Zhōngguó	2
中间价 zhōngjiānjià	7
钟 zhōng	9
周末 zhōumò	10
住 zhù	21
住院 zhùyuàn	18
转 zhuǎn	5
赚钱 zhuànqián	19
准备 zhǔnbèi	9
自己 zìjǐ	11
自行车 zìxíngchē	24
字 zì	16
总 zǒng	9
总裁 zǒngcái	12
总是 zǒngshì	20
走 zǒu	12
最 zuì	15
昨天 zuótiān	6
左 zuǒ	21
坐 zuò	4
做 zuò	8

责任编辑：龙燕俐
封面设计：安洪民

经贸初级汉语口语
上册
黄为之 编著

*

©华语教学出版社
华语教学出版社出版
（中国北京百万庄路24号）
邮政编码 100037
电话: 86-010-68995871 / 68326333
传真: 86-010-68326333
电子信箱: hyjx@263.net
北京外文印刷厂印刷
中国国际图书贸易总公司海外发行
（中国北京车公庄西路35号）
北京邮政信箱第399号 邮政编码100044
新华书店国内发行
1999年（大32开）第一版
2002年第二次印刷
（汉英）
ISBN 7-80052-705-0 / H·774(外)
9-CE-3325PA
定价：23.00元